PRAISE FOR THE PASSION TEST:

"The Passion Test™ provides the simplest, clearest way to get started on knowing what you want—by getting clear on who you are."
—from the Foreword by T. Harv Eker, #1 *NY Times* best-selling author, *Secrets of The Millionaire Mind*

"The Passion Test™ has given me incredible insight into what was missing in my life, where I was not 100% spot on in pursuing my passions. It's simple, it's easy, and it's profound. Out of it came the creation of an organization I'd been putting off for six years and a fuller expression of my love and my commitment to my family. I think there's nothing more important than that."
—Jack Canfield, co-creator of the #1 *NY Times* best-selling series, *Chicken Soup for the Soul*®

"Chris and Janet Attwood have provided a clear, simple, and effective method to help you identify your core passions so you can create the fulfilling life you deserve."
—John Gray, PhD, #1 *NY Times* best-selling author of *Men Are From Mars, Women Are From Venus*

"Quite frankly I was blown away. *The Passion Test*™ is a very direct, practical roadmap on how to become prosperous, how to take what it is you love, and make it into a very, very substantial, and very fulfilling income."
—Bill Harris, Director Centerpointe Research Institute

"Simple, clear, powerful. *The Passion Test*™ is a remarkable tool for getting the clarity you need to begin living your dreams."
—Marci Shimoff, co-author of the #1 NY *Times* best sellers *Chicken Soup for the Woman's Soul* and *Mother's Soul*

"Whether your life purpose is clear or you want to be clearer, *The Passion Test*™ provides a powerful tool for putting you on track to a more fulfilled, more complete life. The clearer your passions—the surer are your chances of realizing them."
—Dr. Pankaj Naram, world-renowned Ayurvedic physician, personal pulse reader to the Dalai Lama and Mother Teresa, co-author, *Secrets of Natural Health*

"The Test itself is an incredibly valuable tool for clarifying what's really important to you in your life. Equally valuable were the lessons Chris and Janet Attwood share for actually living your mission."
—Catherine Lanigan, author, *Romancing the Stone* and *Jewel of the Nile*

"There's absolutely no reason why everyone can't have the life they choose. You can create your life exactly as you want, but not if you're sacrificing your life's energy for something other than what you're most passionate about. I haven't found any process, that will bring you absolutely to the place of your passion, more quickly, more easily and with more fun than *The Passion Test*™."
—Paul Scheele, Chairman Learning Strategies Corporation

"I was amazed at the process—the simplicity and power of it. It has supported me in being much clearer in my daily priorities—brilliant!"

—D. C. Cordova,
CEO and co-founder, Excellerated Business Schools

"If you really want to have, do, be your passion—this is the guide for you. Janet and Chris have devised a powerful system that absolutely works!"

—Dr. Cheryl Clark, Founder Doing Life International, Inc.
and Director, Shock Incarceration and
the Willard Drug Treatment Campus (DTC)
New York Department of Correctional Services

"I've been around a while. I've been speaking, consulting and training for over 25 years, and I had a chance to take *The Passion Test*™. Even though I work on myself continually, I realized that two of my top five passions in life weren't getting focused on, and now I can make some adjustments about how I decide and choose to live life on purpose."

—Scott deMoulin, Destiny Training Systems

"Great work Janet and Chris! Your fast moving and illuminating book *The Passion Test*™ will certainly inspire its readers and help them discover and act upon their unique calling and mission as well as express their inner magnificence. I love the quotes, the stories and the message. Thanks for helping us all do what is most important—live our heartfelt dreams."

—Dr. John F. Demartini, author, *The Breakthrough Experience:
A Revolutionary New Approach to Personal Transformation*

THE PASSION TEST

*The Effortless Path
to Discovering Your Destiny*

♥

JANET BRAY ATTWOOD
and
CHRIS ATTWOOD

THE PASSION TEST:

THE EFFORTLESS PATH TO DISCOVERING YOUR DESTINY

Published by 1stWorld Publishing
1100 North 4th St. Suite 131, Fairfield, Iowa 52556
tel: 641-209-5000 • fax: 641-209-3001
1stworldpublishing.com
book@thepassiontest.com
http://www.thepassiontest.com
The Passion Test is a trademark of Enlightened Alliances

Second Edition

Library of Congress Control Number: 2006902043
SoftCover ISBN: 1595408355
HardCover ISBN: 1595408371
eBook ISBN: 1595408363

This material has been written and published solely for educational purposes. The author and the publisher shall have neither liability nor responsibility to any person or entity with respect to any loss, damage or injury caused or alleged to be caused directly or indirectly by the information contained in this book.

The characters and events described herein are provided from memory. They are intended to be enjoyed and to teach rather than be an exact factual history.

Layout by Liz Howard Graphics
lizhowardgraphics@yahoo.com

Book Cover Design by Foster Covers
www.fostercovers.com

Interviews in Part 2 are included with permission from
Healthy Wealthy nWise, LLC.

My Lord
Thank you for every moment in our lives
Thank you for all you have given us

We are, because of you
Whatever we do, think have or feel
Is because of you.

May we be vessels
Through which you speak.
Use us in ways you desire
As your humble servants
Walking this path hand in hand with you.

May the words on these pages
Touch the hearts of all those yearning
For union with you.
May they inspire each of us
To align our lives with you and your will for us.

All we have,
We offer in gratitude.
We bow to you.

CONTENTS

Foreword by T. Harv Eker   xiii

Introduction   xvii

Part One
DISCOVERING YOUR PASSIONS

1	The Beginning of the Beginning	1
2	The Passion Test is Born	9
3	Taking The Passion Test	15
	Passion Test Guidelines	22
	Passion Test Instructions	27
4	Creating Your Passionate Life	31
	Your Passion Score	35
	Your Passion Cards	37
5	Creating Your Markers	41
6	Allowing the Dream to Come Alive	57
	Your Vision Board	62
	Your Passion Pages	64
	Your 100th Birthday	66
7	The World is As You Are	71
	The Appreciation Game	75
	The 7 Keys to Living Life Aligned with Passion	78
	It Was the Best Experience of My Life	82
	Illustration: Map of Janet's Trip to India	100

Part Two
THE PASSIONS OF REAL LIFE LEGENDS

8   Richard Paul Evans
     Failure Is Not An Option   105

9   Jay Abraham
     It's About Everyone Else   121

10   Dr. Denis Waitley
     Play to Win From Within   139

11   Stephen M. R. Covey
     Moving at the Speed of Trust   153

12   Debbie Ford
     Resigning as General Manager of the Universe   175

13   Dr. John Hagelin
     United At Our Core   191

     Epilogue   203

     Are You Ready for the Next Step?   206
     Resources   211
     Acknowledgements   223
     About the Authors   227
     How to Order   229
     Special Gifts   230

*"There are two great days
in a person's life—
the day we are born
and the day we discover why."*

—William Barclay

FOREWORD

Do you ever feel discouraged and frustrated with your life? Do you ever feel like your dreams will never become reality? Well, this book will change that for you.

Who of us doesn't know living our passion is the key to a happy and fulfilled life? The trick for many people, though, is figuring out what your passion really is.

I've often said, "The number-one reason people don't get what they want is—they don't know what they want."

The Passion Test™ provides the simplest, clearest way to get started on knowing what you want—by getting clear on who you are. As you make your list of ten or fifteen qualities of your ideal life, you'll be surprised to discover what it is that's really important to you.

Clarity is critical to success. Clarity leads to power—the power to act—which is the basis of achievement, fulfillment, and happiness in life. Without a clear direction you are either paralyzed or running around in circles. Worse, you can never reach your full potential, because you dare not fully commit.

Not just any direction will do, and therein lies the challenge. Each of us is unique. Each of us has something special to offer the world. Each of us has our own natural gifts and talents. To be truly happy we must use our uniqueness to add value to the lives of others.

The Passion Test™ which you'll take as you read this book, helps you discover your unique gift, then it's up to you to give it to those who need you.

For your freedom,
T. Harv Eker
CEO and President, Peak Potentials Training
#1 New York Times Best-selling Author,
Secrets of the Millionaire Mind

THE PASSION TEST

———————— ♥ ————————

"How was your trip?" Chris asked.

"It was absolutely the best and most amazing experience of my entire life." Janet replied.

"What happened?"

A perplexed expression came over Janet's face.

"I must be flippin' crazy!" she said.

We'll hear Janet's incredible story before this book is done. But first…

INTRODUCTION

What does it mean to live a passionate life? Exciting, fulfilling, thrilling, on fire, purposeful, turned on, motivated, entertaining, easy, fun, unstoppable. It's a life aligned with destiny.

We all know we'd like to feel our life is purposeful. We all want to be passionate about what we're doing, to be excited about how we spend our days, to love our life and to feel we're making some valuable contribution.

Yet how do you discover what it is that is your real passion? That's what this book is about.

Before we begin we have a few things to discuss with you:

1. The key to creating anything you want in your life

2. A little about who we are

3. The "inner work" this book guides you through and why it's critical to your success

4. How destiny and passion go together.

So, let's get to it.

INTENTION—ATTENTION—NO TENSION

Our friend and advisor, Bill Levacy, shared this piece of wisdom with us. We recommend you make it your mantra. It's the essence of what's required to create anything you want in your life.

Intention – Consciously stating what you choose to create in your life is the first step to manifesting it.

Attention – Your life becomes like that on which you put your attention. Give attention to that which you choose to create in your life and it will begin to show up.

No Tension – When you are open to what is appearing in this moment, you allow God's will to move through you. When you hold tightly to your concepts of how things should be, you shut off the flow of life, which in turn prevents you from enjoying the fulfillment of living your personal destiny.

WHO ARE WE?

If we were you, we'd be wondering, who are these people to be talking about how to live your passion? We used to be married and are no longer. However, we remain best friends and business partners. We have given The Passion Test™ to thousands of people all over the world with phenomenal results. We share it with you now and look forward to hearing your comments after you've taken the Test in Chapter 3.

Janet created The Passion Test™ when she was in her thirties. She followed her dreams, got sidetracked, got back to pursuing her dreams, then got sidetracked again, a number of times.

Chris went through the same kind of thing. It's not unusual for most of us to get excited and passionate, and then feel we have to "be responsible" or we have a concept of what will make us happy (like "getting married") and so we get off track for a while.

Some people stay off track their whole lives. In the hope we can help you get on track, or confirm the track you're on, we have written this book.

In her search for her role in life, in the '70's Janet managed kitchens and hotels for thousands of people in Spain and Italy. She became the top salesperson in job after job and owned two of her own successful businesses (one of them was rated among the top ten companies in her area). She worked for a success seminar company teaching motivational courses. She managed the telemarketing division for Books are Fun, the third largest book buyer in the U.S., which was sold to Reader's Digest for $360 million (the year after her division performed at record levels). Janet also lived for twenty-five years in a meditating community and meditation has always been the basis of her life.

During his career, Chris managed ten different businesses as President, General Manager or Chief Operating Officer. In 1981, after rising to become President of a secondary dealer in government securities, he decided to follow his passions and retire from the world for ten years.

He spent those years in deep meditation, and studied the Vedic literature of India.

In November, 2000, Janet got a call from Mark Victor Hansen, co-author of the phenomenally successful *Chicken Soup for the Soul®* series. Mark and Janet had become friends some years before while Janet was at Books are Fun.

On this call, Mark said, "I'm working on a new book with Robert G. Allen, who wrote the best-selling financial book of all time, *Nothing Down*. I want you to work with us on promoting our new book."

Needless to say, Janet was thrilled. Mark explained what they had in mind. Then he asked her to put together a business plan and get it to him in three days. She describes how she felt:

• • •

I was so excited when Mark called, then he mentioned a business plan, and my heart sank. This is not what I do. It was at that moment inspiration struck.

My ex-husband, Chris, and I had continued to be good friends and stay in regular touch after our divorce. Chris has an MBA and is brilliant when it comes to things like business plans. His skills are also a perfect complement to mine and I thought maybe we could do this project together.

I called him up in California, laid out the scenario for him and asked if he could help me put together a business plan in the next three days. He loved the idea of working with Mark and Bob, but he didn't love the idea of preparing a business plan in such a short time. He told me it would take at least three weeks and he was way too busy with his own work to write it up.

I appealed to his beautiful heart: "Couldn't you do it as my Christmas present?"

Being the remarkably flexible person he is, Chris said OK, he would draft an outline of a business plan which could provide the basis for our next call with Mark and Bob.

That was the beginning of an incredible partnership. Chris and I worked for a year with Mark and Bob creating The Enlightened Millionaire Program, and as we worked with hundreds of people in that program I once again discovered what it means to live life with passion.

♦ ♦ ♦

During that year we began teaching *The Passion Test*™ and discovered what a profound effect it has on people. Over the past five years we've given the Test to people in many different parts of the world, and it's been thrilling to hear the impact it's had on people's lives. Here are a few examples:

It wasn't until I took The Passion Test™ *that I realized one of my five TOP passions was to travel to foreign countries with my two sons. Two days after taking the Test and clarifying my top passions I received an e-mail from my friends inviting me and my two sons to travel to Tonga on their boat to help film a whale expedition. To say the least, my mind was blown! Janet was right when she said, 'that which you put your attention on grows stronger in your life.' I recommend The Passion Test™ for everyone who wants to manifest NOW!*

—Dr. Jacquelyn Buettner

Experiencing The Passion Test™ was truly an awakening experience and created a lasting impression on me. Even though I have done other types of Purpose/Passion work before, The Passion Test™ really clarified things for me and brought a true sense of my values, priorities and passions in life. The Passion Test™…helped me re-focus my direction and it is allowing me to let go of things that have been distracting me from my purpose.

—Terri Tierney

The process is incredible and so valuable for me to find my passion. For many years I have been searching for answers that have for one reason or another eluded me. I can already see that going through [The Passion Test™] has started me on a journey to finally clarify where my passions lie. I am so excited and my energy is just flowing as I begin the next step in the process.

—Dee Berman

You can find more testimonials at:
www.healthywealthynwise.com/pttestimonials

Today we support each other fully in living our passions, whether they make logical sense or not. The result has been a life which is fulfilling beyond anything we could have imagined.

Throughout Part 1 of this book we have woven the story of how Janet is fulfilling one of her passions. She tells her story from her direct experience and we've put it in italics so you can follow it easily. Pay attention to the lessons embedded in this story because those lessons will be critical in helping you fulfill your own destiny.

DOING THE INNER WORK

In our online magazine, Healthy Wealthy nWise, we interview famous transformational teachers every month. Many of these teachers have commented in their interviews that most people don't want to step out of their busy world to take the necessary time to do their "inner homework." Most people are afraid if they stop "doing" then they won't be able to earn a living, take care of their family, pay the mortgage, etc.

Any great teacher will tell you that your results are not created on the gross surface "thinking" or "doing" level of life but from going deep within and tapping into that unbounded reservoir of creativity and intelligence within each of us.

In this book we will share with you some of the core knowledge necessary to live a fulfilled life on every level: personal, emotional, spiritual, physical/material. We believe that everything worth doing always has some element of fun and enjoyment in it.

So in true fun form, we have made this a participatory book, in which we invite you to play with us, dreaming and envisioning your passionate life as you are reading the book. Take an active part in the process as you read, and you will find your personal destiny unfolding effortlessly and irresistibly before you.

WHAT IS PERSONAL DESTINY— DO YOU HAVE ONE?

Of course you do. We all do. Think about it. Not one person on the planet is exactly like anyone else. You are unique. You have unique gifts which no one but you can give. You have those gifts because you have a special role to play in the world which requires giving those gifts.

When you are playing that role, you are living your personal destiny. When you are aligned with your destiny, your life is joyful, delightful, exciting and fulfilling.

Your passions are the loves of your life. They are the things which are most deeply important to you. These are the things which, when you're doing them or talking about them, light you up.

The people whom you love are associated with your passions and, in many cases, your relationship with them may BE your passion. It's not unusual for people to list their spouse or their family or their children among their top passions. For most people, your destiny will be fulfilled as part of a team, and your family is your most fundamental team.

Passion and love are inextricably intertwined because they both arise from the heart. When you follow your passions, you will love your life.

Your passions are not your destiny; they are the clues or keys to your personal destiny. The more passionate your life, the more closely your life is aligned with your destiny.

As you read the interviews with some of the most successful people of our time in Part 2 of this book, you will discover that their sense of destiny arose from the things they felt passionate about.

Destiny is a life's journey. Passions change and morph over time as one comes to know and understand oneself more deeply. As you follow your passions, you will find yourself drawn irresistibly onward until one day, you wake up and find you are living a passionate life, filled with a sense of destiny.

And it begins by getting clear about your top passions, which you'll do before you finish reading this book.

There is a simple formula for living your personal destiny:

Intention—Attention—No Tension

Our contention, without pretension, is that by the end of this book you'll have complete retention about how to manifest your dreams.

Let's hold the intention together that as you read you'll uncover your true passions, and begin living the life you were put here to live.

♥

Part One

DISCOVERING YOUR PASSIONS

1

THE BEGINNING
OF THE BEGINNING!

When you follow your bliss...
doors will open where you would not have thought
there would be doors; and where
there wouldn't be a door for anyone else.

—Joseph Campbell

"How was your trip?" Chris asked.

"It was absolutely the best and most amazing experience of my entire life." Janet replied.

"What happened?"

A perplexed expression came over her face.

"I must be flippin' crazy!" she said. "I got so sick I could hardly move out of bed for a week. I fell off a mountain and almost got killed. I practically froze to death in the Himalayas, got kicked by a donkey and had to travel by myself in India, something I swore I'd never do."

In spite of all this, Janet's trip to India was the best experience of her life. She met more than sixty "Saints," individuals revered for their wisdom and enlightenment. Of these, she interviewed more than forty for her upcoming documentary and book, *The Saints Speak Out*. She trekked to the source of the holy river Ganges, high in the Himalayan mountains, and she had some of the most profound insights of her life.

In a little while we'll tell you more about how Janet's passion created this life-changing trip and the remarkable experiences which came out of it, but first let's talk about the loves of *your* life.

Why are you reading this book? You must have a deep feeling inside somewhere that you have a personal destiny which is more or different than what you are living right now.

Or maybe you just want a happier, more fulfilling life.

We feel fortunate and grateful to have discovered how to live life immersed in our passions.

It's taken a while, over thirty years in the working world for each of us and much of that wasn't easy. We wouldn't be surprised if you know exactly what it feels like to work for weeks, months, or years doing everything you can to get yourself out of the 9 to 5, just getting by, living from paycheck to paycheck life.

Maybe you've attended seminars, or watched TV programs on making money in real estate, or in stocks, or in your own business. Maybe you've tried to make extra money in multi-level marketing, or selling things on eBay, or getting a part time job.

Maybe you know what it's like when yet another great plan fails, when that feeling of depression and discouragement rises up and overwhelms you, turning your insides out and making you wonder, "Is all this really worth it?"

We've been there too. We've discovered those feelings come up when you are not aligned with your personal destiny. And it can all change in a moment, as it did for Janet.

THE LIGHT GOES ON

Janet began her journey dancing under the streetlights as a child...

• • •

I was only about eight years old at the time. I used to lie in bed at night waiting for everyone in my family to go to sleep.

I would then quietly sneak outside and enter my imaginary world. This was my favorite time of day. Underneath the corner street light, my world became a brightly lit stage. It was here that I revealed my deepest desires, always pretending the same thing: I was a beautiful, world-famous actress performing to thousands of ardent admirers. Into the quiet of the early morning, I would sing and dance with total abandon. There on my street corner stage, I felt truly alive and free.

Whenever my aunts and uncles came to visit, I always made sure Dad had me dance and sing for them. How my sister and brother hated me whenever my father gathered everyone in the living room for my Broadway show! At that moment, Mickey and Johnny would run out the back door in total embarrassment.

After all, I couldn't sing on key and I didn't know how to dance. Yet my love for performing in front of anyone far outweighed any insecurity I might feel in the talent department. Without a moment's hesitation, I would entertain anyone who came to visit.

When I was about ten, my dad and I had a talk about a dramatic arts school nearby called Pasadena Playhouse. My best girlfriend down the street attended this school, and I had been begging and pleading with my parents to let me go there too. Their reply had always been the same, "Sorry honey, but we just don't have the money for that sort of thing."

Now, when my Dad was finally making more money and agreeing to my long-standing request, I felt it was no longer in the realm of possibility. Brokenhearted, I looked at my father and said, "I'd love to go

Pasadena Playhouse, but it's just too late. I'm afraid I'm already too old." I thought since I was now older than Shirley Temple when she started acting, I had obviously waited too long and blown my chance at stardom. It puzzled me that my parents didn't recognize this fact as well!

So, in that fateful moment, my fantasy world collapsed and I entered into a world of harsh, hard realities.

Neither my brother nor sister would ever be caught playing make-believe under the early morning streetlights. It was time I grew up and saw I was just too old for that sort of thing.

And that's where I was wrong.

I've always been gifted with the ability to connect heart to heart with others in almost no time. In the working world that has served me well as I was the top salesperson in virtually every job I took. Except the first one.

By the time I turned eighteen I had stopped dreaming and started living a rather uninspired version of "real life." There was never a thought about what I loved to do, hoped to do, or even wanted to do. All that was long forgotten.

When I needed a job, I just scanned the classifieds. My only questions were: How hard would I have to work, and how much was the pay?

In 1981 I started working for a technical recruiting company in San Jose, California, in the heart of Silicon Valley in its heyday, hunting for "disk drive engineers." My employer was enjoying huge success. There was a bell that rang whenever someone made a placement, and it rang many times each day.

Unfortunately, it never rang for me. I watched placement after placement being made, everyone congratulating everyone else, new cars and houses being bought, wonderful vacations being taken—while I just sat at my desk waiting for the clock to strike five. Every day I left work humiliated, angry, embarrassed, depressed, and broke. And every day

I was there, it got worse.

I was hired by an elite, profitable, twelve person company for a very simple reason: almost everyone who worked there was a friend of mine. When a vacancy came up in the company, my friends all agreed, "this is the perfect job for Janet." And why not? I was known to all as a great connector, a networker, a communicator, a real dynamo of energy, someone who could get anything done.

What wasn't known about me, however, was I had absolutely no "left brain," engineer-like capabilities. It never occurred to anyone (including me) that I wouldn't be able to communicate at all with prospective disk drive engineers.

One day I happened to see a flyer for a motivational course called "Yes to Success." A strange awareness came over me. I knew I had to take that seminar. I had no hesitation about calling in sick.

The course leader for the seminar was a young woman named Debra Poneman, whose key point was the importance of "finding your passion."

As I watched Debra teach the class, excitedly discussing ideas like time management and goal setting, I was less interested in what she was saying than in who she was being.

She was clearly living her passion—and it showed in her every word and gesture. Debra definitely appeared to be a truly happy person. There she was, the "ideal woman," uplifting everyone not only with her profound understanding, but also with the love she radiated. At the same time, she was traveling the world, making money talking about what she loved, and doing it all so brilliantly.

Debra taught us when we saw a person who had something we wanted, we needed to move beyond envy or resentment. Instead, we should just tell ourselves, "That's for me!"

I took that advice to heart as I watched Debra. Closing my eyes, I silently repeated my new golden mantra: *That's for me! That's for me! That's for me!*

By a stroke of wonderful good fortune, I was able to drive Debra to the airport when the course ended. As we were waiting for her plane, she stared straight into my eyes and said, "What is your dream, Janet?"

Staring right back at her, I said, "I'm glad you asked! I was just thinking today that you should either hire me or move over, because I am going to be the most successful transformational speaker on the planet."

Just then there was an announcement that the plane was ready for boarding. Without commenting at all on what I had just said, Debra gave me a hug, turned quickly, and walked off. All I could think was, "She hasn't seen the last of me!"

Once I find the direction I really want to go, I'm the kind of person who can make changes very quickly. The next day I returned to work knowing my days as an uninspired drone were about to come to an end. One thought burned in my mind: How could I convince Debra to hire me?

Finally I came up with a plan I knew would impress her. At the end of her course, Debra passed out her schedule of appearances for the coming months, which included New York, Boston, Washington, DC, Fairfield, Iowa; and Los Angeles.

Somehow, I decided, I would get enough money, fly to every one of those places, and sit in the front row of each and every class. Whenever Debra walked into the room, she would see me sitting there and know I meant business—especially after the third or fourth course. The only thing I needed was enough money for all the expenses involved in following Debra around.

That night I met a friend at the local Transcendental Meditation® center I used to frequent. When she casually asked what I had been doing recently, I startled her by loudly and passionately declaring I had finally discovered my purpose on this planet.

I told her about my plan to attend all of Debra's classes.

The following evening, the same friend met me again at the TM center. As we were getting up from meditation, she opened her purse, showered ten crisp one hundred dollar bills on my head, and laughingly said, "Merry Christmas!" I just sat there with my mouth open. As tears came to my eyes, I thanked her for believing in me, and promised that very soon I would repay her incredible generosity.

I followed my plan, going from city to city to each of Debra's seminars. Finally, in Los Angeles, at the last seminar on her schedule, she came up to me and said, "OK, if I can't get rid of you, then I better make use of you. You're hired!"

Needless to say, this was a thrilling moment. I was on my way to my dream. However, as I sat through Debra's seminars, time after time, something much more important happened: the birth of The Passion Test™.

♦ ♦ ♦

♥

2

THE PASSION TEST IS BORN

*I am here for a purpose and that purpose
is to grow into a mountain, not to shrink
to a grain of sand. Henceforth will I apply
ALL my efforts to become the highest mountain
of all and I will strain my potential
until it cries for mercy.*

—Og Mandino

Passion is a very personal experience. Yet when your life is filled with things you are passionate about, when you are doing what you love, your activity takes on a life of its own, pulled irresistibly in directions you can't even begin to imagine.

Through the course of Part 1 of this book we'll share with you the astonishing story of the miracles which appeared in Janet's life, just as a result of gaining clarity about the greatest loves in her life. You'll see that it's not the "how" which is important for you to know, it's the "what." Helping you get clear on the "what" of the passions in your own life is what this book is all about.

As the story of Janet's trip to India unfolds, you'll see how money appeared from nowhere, how her desires came to her, rather than her running after the desires. We'll share the serendipitous events that occurred which she could never have predicted, and how the surface inconveniences or discomforts which inevitably appear along the path of passion, become irrelevant when one is aligned with destiny.

With all that to look forward to, let's return now to Janet's story of the birth of The Passion Test™.

◆ ◆ ◆

On the second day of her seminar, Debra mentioned a survey of one hundred of the most influential, financially successful individuals in the United States. The survey found that each one of these super-successful, powerful people had one thing in common.

"Can any of you guess what that one thing was?" she asked.

We each blurted out what we thought could be the magic answer, but Debra just kept shaking her head.

"What could that one thing be?" I thought.

Finally, after what seemed like forever, Debra said, "The survey found that these powerful, successful people had totally fulfilled those things which they each felt were most necessary for their ideal life."

With that one sentence, my life was changed forever.

In other words, the light went on.

Actually, it was more like fireworks!

Debra continued talking about the importance of knowing what it is you want to be, do, and have; how goal setting is important, then you too could become powerful and successful. It was so easy.

As Debra segued into talking about how to "Dress for Success," I was still in my own world, thinking about the survey.

If those super-successful people were already fulfilling their deepest aspirations, the path to assuring one's own success was obvious. "Clearly what one has to do is determine one's own most important aspirations," I thought.

· · ·

When she got home, Janet sat down and made a list of fifteen of the things she would love to do, be or have in her life.

1. I am a brilliant, successful transformational speaker uplifting humanity all over the world

2. I travel the world first class

3. I am treated like a queen wherever I go

4. I give and receive love in every part of my life

5. I work with an enlightened team

   and the list went on…

She then sorted out her top five. The simple and unique process she used to sort them out is what is now known as The Passion Test™.

To our amazement as we have shared The Passion Test™ with thousands of people all over the world, we have found this simple process is life transforming.

Our main goal in this book is to give you an immediate way to totally align yourself with what it is you are passionate about. The Passion Test™ is for anyone who has a desire to quickly clarify what their passions are, or to verify they are on the right track with their passions.

We'll introduce you to The Passion Test™ in a moment, but first, why is it so important to do what you love?

A friend shared a true story that illustrates the importance of doing what you enjoy perfectly.

It went like this…

A young girl who collected autographs of famous people was at the airport waiting to board her plane when she saw a crowd of people standing around a small man in a white robe.

She knew this man had to be someone well-known because of the large crowd around him. She went up to one of the people standing nearby and asked who the man was. She was told, "that's Maharishi Mahesh Yogi, a great Saint from the Himalayas."

The girl excitedly ran up to Maharishi and immediately asked for his autograph. Maharishi took her pen and paper, looked her straight in the eyes and said, "I will give you something much more important than my autograph." And on the piece of paper he wrote one word.

Enjoy

What was the message Maharishi was conveying? The whole purpose of life is to enjoy. When you are not enjoying you are out of the flow of life. You are missing your purpose.

Again, what's so important about enjoying what you are doing? Think about all the greatest people on the planet, past and present. Every one of them, without exception, loved what they did or are now doing. Every single one of them. Their lives may not have been easy, they certainly faced challenges, and yet, they LOVED what they were doing.

Now think about the people you know who are truly happy. Don't they love what they are doing in their life? Maybe there are some parts of their life which are challenging, but when it comes down to it, they love their life, how they spend their days, and who they spend their lives with, don't they?

For us, it is obvious. To have absolute success in any area, the most important prerequisite must be that you have a passion for doing it.

Do passion and enjoyment go hand in hand? Absolutely! Passion is the inner fire which propels you forward through the combination of love for what you're doing and the inner sense of purpose which comes from connecting to one's deepest passions. Enjoyment arises from this combination of love and purposefulness.

By helping you clarify what you love most, what is most important to you, The Passion Test™ gives you the means to align your life with what you most enjoy.

The Passion Test™ is also powerful because it's a system.

Webster's dictionary defines the word system as:

sys·tem

1. a regularly interacting or interdependent group of items forming a unified whole

2. an organized set of doctrines, ideas, or principles usually intended to explain the arrangement or working of a systematic, an organized or established procedure <the touch system of typing> b : a manner of classifying, symbolizing, or schematizing <a taxonomic system> <the decimal system>

3. harmonious arrangement or pattern : ORDER <bring system out of confusion —Ellen Glasgow>

A system provides order, saves time, requires less energy and costs less. It is an organized, established procedure which produces results, no matter who is using the system.

An easy way to remember the value of a system is the acronym Robert Allen and Mark Victor Hansen coined for system in their book, *The One Minute Millionaire*. S-Y-S-T-E-M=Save Yourself Time Energy and Money.

The Passion Test™ is a system which will help you discover your mission in life. What is your purpose? What is your destiny? What is that work which feels like play no matter how many hours you put into it?

The Passion Test™ is very simple, and don't let that fool you. Its results can be profound. It will give you an easy, fun way to prioritize the things which truly mean the most to you. It will help you eliminate the things which are distractions right now.

The Passion Test™ requires you to face your inner life, and bring it out to the surface so you can examine it to clarify what is really most important to you.

The Passion Test™ is the magical key that will unlock those forgotten dreams which wait patiently in your heart for the day when you are finally ready to say, "I am here to make a difference and the time is Now!"

3

TAKING THE PASSION TEST

God has given each of us
our 'marching orders.'
Our purpose here on Earth is
to find those orders and carry them out.
Those orders acknowledge our special gifts.

—*Soren Kierkegaard*

It was 2003. We had formed Enlightened Alliances, and enjoyed some great successes. Liz and Ric Thompson had approached us with the idea of partnering to create *Healthy Wealthy nWise*, the magazine we now run together. Chris was working on what eventually became our book, *From Sad to Glad*, clarifying the seven step Expansion Process which has allowed us to remain best friends and business partners.

Janet felt it was now time to once again clarify her passions. She had taken The Passion Test™ many times before, but this time was different. Something was stirring inside which she knew was going to have a profound effect on her life.

As she made her list of the things which are most deeply important to her, the things she will be, do or have when her life is ideal, she realized she had more clarity about these things than ever before.

One item on the list jumped out at her: "Spending time with the enlightened." It was as if this short phrase was a spark which ignited an insatiable fire inside of her.

Even as she felt deeply drawn to this idea, she thought, "How in the world will I ever do that?" After all, those who are most revered for their wisdom and enlightenment are either surrounded by huge organizations with lots of people protecting them or hidden away in caves, high in the Himalayas or dense forests.

She knew she wanted to begin by traveling to India, because she had already met some enlightened masters there, but beyond that she had no clue how her passion could possibly get fulfilled.

Before we tell you how Janet's passion for spending time with the enlightened was realized and continues to be, you need to take The Passion Test™ yourself. Just remember, for now, you don't need to figure out HOW any of the things you put on your list of passions will be realized. We'll help you with that once you get your real passions down on paper.

In giving people The Passion Test™, we have found the biggest challenge most people have is getting out of their own way. What we mean by this is that when most people first take The Passion Test™, they start to write a passion and then if they can't immediately see how they can practically manifest it, they erase it, (especially the real big ones!) and put something down that they can put their arms around. In other words, they play it "safe."

For example, maybe you dream of being a multimillionaire. Now from your present income level, that may seem totally unrealistic. So, instead of writing your passion as being a multimillionaire, you "play it safe" and put, "Getting a raise."

We can hear your thoughts now: "But I don't have any idea

how I'm going to become a multimillionaire." Trust us. It doesn't matter. Write it down.

Janet didn't have a clue how she'd be able to spend time with enlightened masters when she wrote down, "spend time with the enlightened." Yet you'll see as her story unfolds, the result was much better than anything she could ever have dreamed up.

Once your intention is clear, attention is the next step. If you think your passion is becoming a multimillionaire, and you don't have any inclination to put your attention on making money and creating wealth, then your mind is playing games with you, telling you this is your passion, when in fact it just wants to be safe from bills, responsibilities and discomfort. Such mind games never lead to fulfillment.

Passions arise from the heart. When you are truly passionate about something, you don't have to try hard to put attention on it. It's fun, it's engaging, it's exciting. When challenges arise, they can't deter you. They may slow you down for a little while, but they can't stop you.

Let's come back to this idea of "playing it safe." Have you ever noticed people who play it "safe" aren't at all as enthusiastic, energetic, full of passion, on fire and excited about their life as your friends who dance around on the edge and totally go for their dreams?

Think about someone you know who always chooses the safe route. When looking for a job, they'll take the lower salary with health insurance, retirement benefits and paid vacation with an established company rather than take the risks in a start up which may pay more, offer stock options, and have a more family-like environment.

Those people don't hike too close to the edge of the cliff, don't jump off the high dive, don't travel to areas where they might encounter some awful disease. They don't live where they'd love to because it costs too much, don't fly in small planes, don't drive at high speeds, don't sail across the ocean, don't do anything that might be dangerous, risky or scary.

Are those the kind of people you want to be like?

On the other hand, what's it like to be someone who goes for the gusto in every moment? What does it feel like to be someone who is doing whatever it takes to live your dream; who is willing to face any challenge, jump through any hoops, go anywhere you have to, in pursuit of your heart's dearest desires?

Don't get us wrong here, we're not going to tell you to jump off the mountain until you're ready, but we do want to impress upon you the importance of thinking of your IDEAL life, not your POSSIBLE life.

There is a secret to sorting out the "how" of your dreams which we will share with you a little later. This secret is revealed in the story of Janet's trip to India, and that trip would never have happened if she hadn't first given herself permission to be open to all possibilities as she clarified the "what."

So, right now, please trust us. Don't censor your Passion Test.

To make sure you are going to set free those BIG PASSIONS that so far might not have yet come out, Janet will share with you an example of the passions list of a friend of hers who has no problem thinking big.

◆ ◆ ◆

A couple of years ago Chris and I were speaking at T. Harv Eker's Wealth and Wisdom seminar in Vancouver. My great friend and associate, Jack Canfield of Chicken Soup for the Soul® fame was also a featured presenter.

At the time I was writing my e-book, The Passion Test™: Discovering Your Personal Secrets to Living a Life on Fire. I wanted to take Jack through the test so I could have it in my book.

I rang Jack up in his hotel room the morning he was leaving for

California and asked if I could meet with him before he left to give him The Passion Test™. Jack said the timing just wouldn't work because he was on his way to the airport and his taxi was waiting.

"No problem," I said, "can I come along and give you the Test on the way?"

I can still hear Jack chuckling through the phone as he said, 'You're a crazy redhead! OK—meet you downstairs.'

On the way to the airport I explained to Jack how The Passion Test™ worked and in about one minute he had shot out fifteen of his greatest passions.

Talk about knowing who you are and what you love!

I wasn't surprised. With over 100 million Chicken Soup for the Soul® *books sold worldwide, obviously the guy knows where he wants to go and he definitely doesn't have a problem thinking big enough.*

Here's Jack's initial list of passions:

1. Being of service to massive numbers of people

2. Having an international impact

3. Enjoying celebrity status

4. Being part of a dynamic team

5. Having a leadership role

6. Helping people live their vision

7. Speaking to large groups

8. Having an impact through television

9. Being a multimillionaire

10. Having world class quarters and support team

11. Having lots of free time to be

12. Studying with spiritual masters regularly

13. Being part of a spiritual leaders network

14. Creating a core group of ongoing trainers who feel identified with his organization

15. Having fun-fun-fun!

Here's what Jack's Test results looked like after I walked him through the elimination process:

1. Helping people live their vision

2. Being part of a dynamic team

3. Being of service to massive numbers of people

4. Having an international impact

5. Creating a core group of ongoing trainers who feel identified with his organization

Just like those very successful people in the study which inspired The Passion Test™, after going through the Test, Jack told me all five of his passions were already completely actualized in his life. But one thing surprised Jack. Passion #13: Being part of a spiritual leaders network— was #6 after the elimination process. Although it was very important to him, this passion was nowhere in Jack's life yet. As we said goodbye, he told me he was going to get started on that one right away.

Sidebar: Today, Chris and I are pleased to be founding members of Jack's "Transformational Leadership Council," a growing group of over sixty speakers, authors and trainers from around the world formed by Jack. He created this group not long after he took The Passion

Test™ and saw that being part of such a network was important to him.

OK, I'm obviously proud of my little test for being part of the birthing of one of Jack's dreams. Enough said.

Now back to Jack's Test...

Notice anything about it?

How about almost every one of his passions is a pretty darn big one, yes?

Was Jack concerned when I gave him the test if he could fulfill his passions? Absolutely not. The next principle I am now going to give you was already encoded in Jack's DNA way before he took the Test.

(By the way, we will repeat these mantras throughout the book until you eat, breathe and drink them and have them encoded in your DNA as well.)

OK, here goes...

> **When you are clear,**
> **what you want will show up in your life,**
> **and only to the extent you are clear.**

The opposite of this is also true: fuzzy desires give fuzzy results. The vast majority of this book is dedicated to helping you achieve greater clarity. We will give you a number of tools to help you clarify your passions as we continue.

◆ ◆ ◆

Now let's review the guidelines for doing your own Test.

PASSION TEST GUIDELINES

The first part of The Passion Test™ as described in the Instructions in the next section is to make a list of your passions, i.e. those things which you love most, which are most important to you, which are most critical to your happiness and well-being.

As you prepare your initial list of passions, play full out; no holding back. Write down at least ten and as many as fifteen or more things which you absolutely love.

Your list will complete the sentence:

When my life is ideal, I am _____

What you're writing here are your passions, not your goals. Passions are how you live your life. Goals are the things you choose to create in your life. For example, one of Jack's passions is "being a multimillionaire." Even if Jack wasn't already a multimillionaire, his passion would be stated as "being a multimillionaire." However, he may have a goal to earn $2 million dollars in the next year.

What's the difference? A passion is how you choose to live your life. Jack chooses to live life as a multimillionaire. A goal is something you aim to achieve. The goal could be stated "To earn $2 million dollars within the next year."

When your passions are clear, then you can create goals which are aligned with your passions and begin to create the life you choose to live.

Both passions and goals are valuable, and the first step is getting clear on your passions.

Think about what you will do, be and have when your life is ideal. As Jack did with his list, begin each passion with a verb which expresses how you are living life when your life is ideal.

Here are examples of passions some of our students have expressed:

- Living in a beautiful home in which I feel completely at peace

- Writing successful mystery novels

- Working in a nurturing environment with lots of plants and light

- Enjoying perfect health with lots of energy, stamina and vitality

- Having fun with everything I do

- Spending lots of quality time with my family

- Enjoying great sex on a regular basis

- Working with a supportive team of people who share my values

Ok, those are all good and fine. What if your passions are altruistic, like having a peaceful world, or eliminating poverty on earth, or eradicating disease?

Remember, passions are how you live your life. Goals are things which you achieve.

Living a life of peace could be a passion. Creating peace in the world is a goal. Living life in abundance could be a passion. Eliminating poverty on earth is a goal.

Now, could someone have a passion for eliminating poverty on earth or ending world hunger? Absolutely. Lynne Twist, a member of the Transformational Leadership Council, is a great example. Lynne spent many years as a fundraiser and leader of The Hunger Project, an international organization which has made a huge impact in eliminating world hunger. Lynne's passion was *working* to end world hunger. The *goal* of The Hunger Project is to end world hunger.

Do you get the difference? Passions are about process. Goals are about outcomes.

As you think about your list of passions, here are some ideas to help get you going:

Loves and Talents: Clues to Your Unique Gifts

What do you love to do? What kind of environment do you love to be in? What kind of people do you love to be around? What excites you, turns you on, gets you charged up? The answers to these questions all provide clues to your purpose.

Here's another set of clues: What are you good at? What do people compliment you on? What do you notice you seem to do better than most others? What are your unique skills and talents?

You most likely enjoy doing the things you're good at, so loves and talents often go together.

Beware the Mind

If that's all there is to it, why do so many people fail to fulfill their life's purpose? Your mind tends to trick you. The mind is like a monkey, jumping here and there and everywhere.

First it's running toward something enticing, then it's running away from something scary. Your mind will even try to convince you your life's purpose is something less than it really is—in the name of safety and security.

For example, many people tell us their passion is to make lots of money. But some of them have no attraction to things which have to do with money, making money, or creating more money.

These people may have a passion for service, or a passion for their family, or a passion for being in nature. There is nothing about making money, per se, which attracts them, turns them on or gets them excited. When we talk to them, what we discover is they don't care so much about having lots of money, as they do about feeling the freedom to do the things they love.

It's not necessary to have lots of money to have that freedom. For example, Mother Theresa had complete freedom to do the things she loved, yet she never personally had lots of money. The same is true of Mahatma Gandhi or Martin Luther King.

On the other hand, we've met some people (Harv Eker comes to mind) who have a burning passion to make lots of money, combined with a passion to help lots of people at the same time. There is nothing which can stop those people from making money. They are so focused on making lots of money that there's no way it can't show up.

Follow your passions, be open to receive support from wherever it may come and you will find fulfillment is growing in your life. If the security and freedom money provides is very important to you, then it will show up.

Making money and creating wealth are learned skills for most people. To have money and wealth requires either investing the time, energy and money to learn those skills, or surrounding yourself with people who have them.

Will the things you're passionate about change somewhat over time? Absolutely. As we learn, grow and evolve, our vision expands. That's why taking The Passion Test™ every few months will help keep you on track to achieving your life's purpose.

The Passion Test™ is a tool to help you understand the key success elements for YOU to live a happy, fulfilled life. It is very personal. Your five will not be exactly the same as anyone else's. Just remember, happy, successful people have all five of their top passions present in their life. The Passion Test™ will help you identify your top five, and put you on the road to a fulfilling life.

A Few Other Guidelines Worth Mentioning

As you make your list, keep the following in mind:

• Don't consult with anyone. This is about the things that light YOUR fire. Go deep inside and connect with the things which are truly most important to you.

• Don't take the Test as a couple. Do the process on your own. Later, if you choose you can share your passions with your spouse or partner. If you really, really want to do it together, then each of you prepare your own initial list, and afterwards take each other through the elimination process. If you do this, DON'T try to influence your partner's choices. It's their test. If you don't like their choices, then think about whether you can love them enough to want for them what they want for themselves.

• We recommend you take the Test in one sitting. It should only take 20 – 30 minutes, unless you really aren't at all clear about what things are most important to you, then it could take a little longer.

• If possible, take the Test in a quiet environment, without distractions. This is a process of going deep within to those things that mean most to you in your life. You won't find them when you're stirred up and having to pay attention to other things.

PASSION TEST INSTRUCTIONS

You can take The Passion Test™ anytime. Just follow the instructions below.

First, make a list of at least ten of the most important things you can think of which would give you a life of joy, passion and fulfillment. Begin each one with a verb relating to being, doing or having which completes the sentence:

When my life is ideal, I am _____

Close your eyes and picture your ideal life. What are you doing? Who are you with? Where are you? How do you feel?

Now make your list and know that this is just your first list. If you follow our advice to take the Test every six months, you'll be doing this many, many times over the coming years, getting clearer every time. Don't censor. You don't need to know the how, just the what.

Make your list now—list at least ten, and as many as you want:

1. _____

2. _____

3. _____

4. _____

5. _____

6. _____

7. _____

8. _____

9. _____

10. _____

11. _____

12. _____

13. _____

14. _____

15. _____

Let your list sit for a while. Come back to it in a few hours or tomorrow. When you return to your list, compare the items on the list to identify which are the most important to you as follows:

a. If you could have #1 or #2, but not both, which would you choose? Keep in mind that in making your choice, you are not losing anything. We ask you to compare the two items as if you could only have one of them. This is necessary in order to get in touch with what is most deeply important to you. In real life you can certainly have both.

b. Continue comparing the one you choose with the next number on the list until you go through the whole list and then label the one you chose as #1. For example, if you compared the first item on the list to the second, and you chose the second, then you would next compare the second item to the third. If you again chose the second item, then you'd compare the second item to the fourth and so on, always comparing your choice to the next item on the list.

c. Start again, compare each item which remains (don't include the ones you've already chosen), always keeping the one that's more important. When you get to the end of the list, label the choice remaining #2. Go through the list again and label the choice remaining #3, and so on until you identify your five most important passions.

d. If you get stuck and can't decide which item is more important, then ask yourself, "If I could be, do or have #1 and not #2 which would bring me more bliss? Or, if I could be #2 and not #1 which would bring me more bliss?" State the choice so that it is clearly an either/or choice in order to be able to choose between them.

e. Most people find their first impulse is the most accurate. Passion arises from the heart, and your heart's impulse is more likely to be closer to the truth than your mind's analysis.

f. Be honest. Don't worry if your choices aren't what others think they should be. You don't have to show this list to anyone else. This is about what lights your fire, right now. The more closely aligned you are with what you truly love, the happier, more fulfilled you will be. The happier you are, the more attractive you will be to those you love and cherish. As a great teacher once said, "Happiness radiates like the fragrance from a flower and draws all good things toward you."

g. Avoid the temptation to get to an item on your list that seems really important to you and say, "Oh, that's number one, so I don't need to go through the rest of the list." We can't begin to tell you how many times we have taken people through the Test, had them say that, then discover things changed as they went through the complete list. So, go through the comparison process with every item on your list for all five of your top passions.

h. Don't be surprised if the choices you make change, each time you go through the list. When you are simple and innocent going through the process without holding on to any agenda, your mind and heart will go deeper each time you go through the list. As this happens, it's not unusual for your choices to change as you continue.

If you want to get an idea of what some others have written for their Passion Test, go to:

http://www.healthywealthynwise.com/ptresults

And what was that mantra which is getting encoded in your DNA?

> **When you are clear,**
> **what you want will show up in your life,**
> **and only to the extent you are clear.**

Magic happens when you are clear. You will find yourself saying, "That was the best experience of my life!" And so it was for Janet as she began thinking about how she would manifest her love for "spending time with the enlightened."

4

CREATING YOUR
PASSIONATE LIFE

*The person born with a talent they
are meant to use will find their greatest
happiness in using it.*

—Johann Wolfgang von Goethe

*Ok...I can do this. After all, I've been networking most of my life and
finding Saints to interview can't be any harder than finding a movie star
or any other famous person.*

"Hmm... let me see. Why would they want to see me anyway?"

*These and similar thoughts went racing through my head as I looked at
this new, #1 passion in my life.*

*"Where do I start with something so far outside of "normal" life?" I
thought.*

*Have you ever been totally perplexed by a problem, challenge or situa-
tion in your life? The more you think about it, the more perplexing it*

becomes. Sometimes the best thing you can do is just forget about it for a while, and that's what I did.

Then one day a friend called. "Janet, there is this wonderful Saint from India coming to Chicago. You should interview him for your magazine."

It was an "Aha" moment.

"That's it! If I write articles for our magazine about enlightened Saints, then I could turn that into a book and these Saints might be willing to spend time with me in order to get their message out. Now that would be fun!" I thought.

A plan began to emerge.

"I'll contact my friends who have lived in India, or traveled there frequently; find out who in India is most revered for their wisdom and knowledge, and see if these Saints will let me interview them." It was a good plan; I just needed a little guidance.

I got on the phone to Bill Levacy, to get his advice on the trip from his expertise in Vedic astrology. He encouraged me to make the trip to India, "Just be sure to take a video camera with you to record your interviews. It doesn't have to be anything fancy, just have the camera there and record your sessions with these Saints."

Another epiphany.

"I'll create a documentary! What more important thing can I do than to bring people throughout the world the insights of the wise regarding what we need to do about the current world situation?" I was on cloud nine, floating in the vision of sitting at the feet of the wisest teachers in the world, when all of a sudden, I came crashing back to the ground.

"This could cost a lot of money, especially the way I like to travel! All of my money is tied up in our business. How will I ever pay for this trip, not to mention the equipment I'll need?" Reality hit hard.

◆ ◆ ◆

We'll tell you how hundreds of thousands of dollars came to Janet in the next few months, but first we need to help you score your passions and create your Passion Cards.

You've identified the five things which you love, which are most important to you in your life right now. Will these change? Absolutely.

We take The Passion Test™ every six months because we know that as our experience of life grows, we come to know ourselves ever more deeply. You may get married, have babies, new opportunities will show up, you will make new discoveries. Life is constantly evolving, and with that evolution comes greater clarity about what is most important.

For example, when Chris first started doing The Passion Test, he was a senior executive for a successful consulting and training company. One of his top five passions was:

"Determining my own hours."

Today, that passion is nowhere to be found on Chris' list. The fact that he has complete control over his own hours could have something to do with that.

However, when you look at his current list, you see his #3 passion is: "Having fun with everything I do." When you talk to him about what this means to him, part of having fun for Chris is having the freedom to do what he wants, when he wants.

The way in which Chris expresses his passion is different today than it was years ago. He's discovered that "Determining my own hours" is just part of a deeper passion, which is "Having fun with everything I do."

The deeper you know yourself, the more completely you are able to align with your personal destiny.

And for right now, you've created the only list which really matters. It's the list of your passions as you know them now. It's time for another mantra:

What you put your attention on grows stronger in your life.

You are constantly creating your life. We all are. We create our life out of the things to which we give attention. And you attract into your life more of what you put attention on.

If your attention is on all the things you don't have, all the problems in your life, all the bad things which are happening to you, then you are creating more of that.

If you want more problems, more challenges, more unhappiness, then give attention to those things. If you want more passion, fulfillment and joy in your life, then give your attention to the things which create these.

People focus on what they don't want out of fear. They're afraid they won't have enough money, or they'll get sick, or there will be a disaster. Out of fear they spend lots of time worrying about all the bad things which could happen in their life.

One of our favorite sayings is: "Fear is vividly imagining exactly what you don't want to happen, happening."

YOUR PASSION SCORE

Would you like a simple way to discover what you've been putting your attention on up until now? Ok, you've twisted our arms, here it is:

Go through the top five passions you identified from your Passion Test and rate each one on a scale of 0 to 10. 0 means you're not living that passion in your life at all. 10 means you are fully living it.

Go ahead and do that now.

Did you notice any significant differences in the scores? Most people do.

The passions which have low scores are the ones you haven't given as much attention to. The passions with high scores have received a lot of your attention.

Could happen that you think you've been giving a lot of attention to something and the score is still low? Possibly. If you think that's the case, look carefully at where your attention has really been.

For example, suppose one of your passions is to own a multi-million dollar business. You've been working on your business for several years, and it's still just getting by, barely supporting you. Doesn't sound like a 10 does it?

So, you say, "I've been putting lots of attention on my business, and it's still just getting by."

Go back and think about what you have really been putting your attention on. Has your attention been fully focused on the tremendous value you are providing to your customers? Have you been fully focused on treating each customer with honor and respect so they go away grateful for having the chance to do business with you? Have you been putting your attention on all the successes and profits which are flowing to you?

Or has your attention gone to all the bills you have to pay? Or how unreasonable some customers are? Or how little you have left over at the end of each month? Or how deeply in debt you are?

When we say, "What you put your attention on grows stronger in your life," we don't mean that putting attention on something in some generalized, fuzzy, non-specific way will make the things you want appear in your life. We mean what you give attention to, every moment of every day, day in and day out, determines what is created in your life.

If your attention is on all the things you can't have and can't do, then you won't have them and you won't be able to do them. If your attention is on the benefits, blessings and good fortune which is flowing into your life, then you will find more and more of those things showing up.

If you are really honest with yourself, you will discover where you put your attention is creating the results you are experiencing in your life.

The great news is where you put your attention is primarily a habit. Given about twenty-one days of consistently applying a new behavior, you can change any habit. All that is required is the will to make the change.

If you find you're having trouble changing a habit of thinking about the problems, difficulties or challenges in your life, we recommend the "Rubber Band" technique.

Get a rubber band and put it on your wrist. Wear it seven days a week, 24 hours a day for at least thirty days.

Every time you have a thought which you know is not creating what you want in your life, pull the rubber band out away from your wrist and let it snap back against your skin. Ouch!

Yes, you'll feel it. And that tactile reminder will help train your mind that these types of thoughts don't serve you.

Do this for a month and you'll find you have taken a big step in breaking the habit of putting your attention on things which create unhappiness and failure in your life.

YOUR PASSION CARDS

Since you're now committed to putting your attention on your passions, we'll share a proven method for creating whatever you want in your life.

Some years ago when we were partners with Mark Victor Hansen and Robert Allen, Janet was in Phoenix, Arizona at an event where the well-known motivational speaker, Bob Proctor, was presenting. She tells the story:

• • •

One of the first things Bob said when he got up to speak was, "Do you know how easy it is to be wealthy? I currently have more than four hundred multiple streams of income—and it's all because of this little card."

He reached into his coat, withdrew a file card, and showed it to the group. It said, "I am thankful and happy for the following…" and it listed his five goals in priority order.

Bob explained that the mind is like a computer: Whatever you input into the mind has to get printed out or show up in your universe sooner or later. Most people spend their time putting their attention on what they lack, instead of what they choose to create, and so they get more lack.

As he held up his small card, Bob had an infectious smile on his face when he said to the group, "One of the most important parts of my day is spent looking at this little card."

He explained he put file cards with his goals in strategic places so he could easily glance at them from time to time during his day. As soon as one goal was fulfilled, he replaced it with a new one.

"It's that easy," he said.

• • •

Now it's time to put Bob's advice into practice as applied to your passions.

Get a number of 3" x 5" cards. Write your passions on each card like this:

MY PASSION TEST

Date: ___/___/___

I am so happy and thankful that I am now living
my passions and drawing the following into my life:

1. _____

2. _____

3. _____

4. _____

5. _____

THIS OR SOMETHING BETTER!

What was that last little line at the bottom?

"This or something better!" In our experience, the Universe almost always has a better plan in mind for us than what we can think up, as long as we're open to receive it. Soon you'll see an example of how that's true when we tell you how Janet's passion of being with the enlightened got fulfilled.

Here's a sure-fire rule which is guaranteed to lead you to living a passionate life:

> *Every time you're faced with a decision,*
> *choose in favor of your passions.*

In order to choose in favor of your passions, you have to remember what they are, at the time you are making a decision. How do you do that? Repetition.

Put the 3" x 5" cards up where you will see them several times a day. What are good places?

- Your bathroom mirror so you see your passions first thing in the morning

- By your computer so you see your passions while you're writing emails

- In your purse or wallet so you can refer to them at any time during the day

- In your car on the dashboard so you see them when you are going places

- On the refrigerator so you see them while preparing meals or getting snacks

The purpose of posting these cards is to keep your attention easily on your passions. You don't have to study the cards. You don't have to concentrate on them. You don't have to create plans to figure out how to live them (although there is nothing wrong with that when you feel inspired).

What you need to do is read through your passions several times a day so they become deeply ingrained. So deeply ingrained that whenever you are faced with a decision you can ask yourself: Is this going to help me be more aligned with my passions or less aligned?

Writing out your Passion Cards and posting them is your most important first step in creating your passionate life. So, go post your cards now and be open to receive the unexpected in your life.

5

CREATING YOUR MARKERS

> We are at our very best, and we are happiest,
> when we are fully engaged in work we enjoy, on
> the journey toward the goal we've established for
> ourselves. It gives meaning to our time off and
> comfort to our sleep. It makes everything else in
> life so wonderful, so worthwhile.
>
> —Earl Nightingale

"Why are you packing two big suitcases when you are only going to Santa Barbara for four days?" Chris asked.

"I know. Pretty weird, huh?" I replied. "I'm just too tired to think about what I need, and it really doesn't matter. It's always nice to have choices. You never know what could come up. You know me, I like to be ready for anything."

I was on my way to Santa Barbara, California to meet Jack Canfield and other well-known writers and speakers for the first meeting of the Transformational Leadership Council.

While there, I took some time with my dear friend, Christian. When we went out to lunch, I shared my plan to create a documentary.

"I've never used a video camera in my life." I told Christian. "I'd love to hire a professional to come and do the filming for me."

"Do you know anyone?" she asked.

"There is one woman I really like named Juliann whom I met several years ago. I think she has done production or editing in Hollywood for some time, but I haven't talked with her in a couple of years."

Brrrrrng, brrrrrrng. It was my cell phone.

"Hello?"

"Hi Janet? This is Juliann Jannus." Hearing Juliann's voice I almost dropped my cell phone in my salad!

I told Juliann about the incredible serendipity that after not being in contact for several years, she would call me at the exact moment I was telling Christian about her.

"I've got chills," Juliann said.

"Me too!" I replied.

"So how did you find me?" I asked.

"Right now I'm driving down the freeway in San Diego with my friend Stephanie. We're on our way to the Prince concert and were just talking about what's going on in our lives. Stephanie tells me she is going to India and when I asked her who with, she said, 'Janet Attwood.'

"I told her, 'Janet Attwood—I love Janet Attwood. Lets call her right now!'"

In thinking about ways to finance my trip to India, I planned a tour for women to some of the famous spiritual spots in that spiritual land. It turned out one of the women who had signed up to come was a friend of Juliann's.

I had to find out if this was the answer to my prayers, so I asked, "Look

Juliann, I don't know what you are up to, but is there any chance you'd want to go to India with me and film Saints?"

As it turned out, Juliann was completely bored with her present work situation and going to India sounded like just the adventure she felt she needed. I told her once I got home I would call her and we would continue making the necessary plans.

On the day I was to leave Santa Barbara I woke up in the morning with the clearest intuition I wasn't supposed to leave California yet. I called Chris to let him know my plans.

"Chris, I've changed my ticket for a month out."

"You what?" Chris asked, not sounding at all happy about my new plan. "Why did you do that?"

"I don't know actually. I just woke up and had the strongest feeling not to go yet.

"Look, since I have my computer and my cell phone, it's no biggy, I can do all of my work from here. You won't mind watching the doggies for me will you?"

Chris has always been incredibly supportive of my sometimes inexplicable decisions. He tells me he's learned to trust my intuitions because they always seem to have some good outcome, even if I can't explain why that happens.

After Chris said he'd look after my dogs I then called my brother John in San Diego to tell him I was coming to spend time with him and our stepmom, Margie.

"Well, Margie's at the hospital right now. No big deal. Just routine tests. She'll be out today, I know she'd love to see you," John said.

"Ok, I'll take the Amtrak down. I have some emails to catch up on and going along the coast will be fun." I got John to give me the number of the hospital where Margie was getting her tests so I could call and let her know I was coming.

When I called the hospital, they put me through to her doctor.

"I'm so sorry," the doctor said when he heard I was Margie's stepdaughter. "Margie has been diagnosed with terminal cancer and has decided to forego any treatment. Because we can no longer help her, someone will need to come pick her up and take her home immediately.

"How long does she have?" I asked, in shock.

"About five to six months. Will you be the one who will be coming for her?" he replied.

• • •

You can never know what will show up in your life. You can only stay open to what is required of you in the present moment. When you let go of the way YOU think things should be, and open yourself to the way they are appearing, you open yourself to the will of God, to the perfect organizing power of Nature.

That's what Janet did and we'll tell you about the amazing miracles which occurred as a result, but first we need to help you create your Markers.

Markers are one more step in gaining increasing clarity.

Dr. Pankaj Naram is a famous Ayurvedic physician, personal pulse reader for the Dalai Lama, and one of our dear friends. Many years ago when Pankaj was in his twenties he was, in his words, "a nobody, who knew nothing, and had nothing."

At that time, his teacher asked Pankaj what was the number one most important thing to him in his life. Pankaj said, "To be the most renowned Ayurvedic physician in the world, making Ayurveda available to people throughout the world."

His teacher told him, "OK, then write it down." Pankaj wrote it down and his teacher then asked him, "How will you know when you are living this dream?"

Pankaj thought for a few minutes and said, "I will take the pulse of at least 100,000 people, Mother Theresa will come to my clinic and acknowledge my work, I will take the pulse of the Dalai Lama, and I will have Ayurvedic centers all over the world."

His teacher said, "Ok, write it down." Pankaj thought to himself, "How will I, a nobody, ever accomplish any of these things," but he loved and respected his teacher so he wrote them down.

Now, more than two decades later, Pankaj has taken the pulse of over 400,000 people, Mother Theresa did come to his clinic in the 80's and praised him for the great AIDs work he is doing, he is now called on to take the pulse of the Dalai Lama, and he has Ayurvedic centers in twelve countries around the world.

How did this happen?

Everything made by man is created first in someone's mind, then it becomes manifest in the world. Look around the room where you are sitting right now.

See that lamp? It began with Thomas Edison's idea that electricity can be used to heat a filament which will then produce light. Then someone else had the thought, "Let me design this beautiful (or practical) lamp in which a light bulb can be put." Someone else had the thought, "How can we make thousands of these, distribute them to thousands of people and make a good profit?" Then you had the thought, "I like this lamp. It will look nice in our house."

Through all these thoughts the lamp in your room got to you. Starting just as an idea, it eventually became a concrete reality in your life.

Every single thing you can see which was created by man was an idea in someone's mind at one time. If you want to create the life of your dreams, it begins by writing your dreams down and getting as clear as possible about them.

The power of intention and attention is what brings ideas into concrete form in the world. When you have intention and attention with no tension, then the whole process becomes fun.

Intention is the conscious or unconscious choice to create.

All of us are creating the circumstances and situations in our world constantly by virtue of the beliefs and concepts we hold as true.

For most people, their creations are unconscious and so they view themselves as the victims of their situations and circumstances.

However, successful people know the secret—they create their reality from what they put their attention on. In this book, we use "intention" to mean the conscious choices you make to create your world.

Some people state intentions and then are perplexed when the results in their life don't match their stated intentions. Why would that happen?

Here is a secret which could be worth millions of dollars and a lifetime of fulfillment to you, so pay close attention:

Your results will ALWAYS match your true intentions.

Another way of saying this is that your life will always express what is going on deep inside you. Therefore, if your results are out of line with your stated intentions, it's time to do some self-examination.

Does this mean "bad" things don't happen to "good" people? Will pure intentions keep you from being trapped in a hurricane, or your house destroyed by fire? Let's assume the answer is no.

Imagine two people are trapped in rising floodwaters from a huge storm. One is intent on ensuring his own survival and is giving his full attention to all the threats to his life. He doesn't care about anyone else. He may even save himself at the expense of others.

The other is intent on giving love and helping those around her. Her full attention is on how she can give her love, her support, and her assistance to the people with whom she is trapped in this situation.

How do you think each will experience their lives in the midst of this catastrophe? The first is filled with fear, thinking about himself, and desperate to save himself.

The second is so immersed in helping others that all she experiences is the love that is flowing between her and those she is assisting. She doesn't have time to worry and fret about the dangers, because her attention is focused on giving, and receiving, love.

Will she be saved? Wouldn't you do everything in your power to save such a person? And whether she survives or not, what are the results in her life? She provides and receives comfort. She is filled with love. She gives and receives help. She enjoys a quality of life which transcends the significance of physical survival.

In a more mundane example, some years ago we partnered with some friends to create a business. Together we stated our intention to generate $10 million in revenues and over $2 million in profits the first year. We created a detailed plan and we were convinced we'd be successful.

A year later we were $100,000 in debt after generating $1 million in revenues. What happened?

We stated our intentions clearly, we made a detailed plan, we executed the plan, and we worked our tails off. What went wrong?

When we looked back over that time later, we realized our REAL intention was to make our partners happy by agreeing to what they wanted. There were many times we felt something should be done differently, but because we believed they were more experienced in that arena, we decided it wasn't our place to change the way things were done.

In the short term, we did make them happy. We did things they liked, but in the end all of us were disappointed in the results.

Your results will ALWAYS match your true intentions.

This means if you want to know what is going on at the

deepest level of your life, look to your results. When your results are out of line with your stated intentions, look more deeply to discover your real intentions and then work on changing those to change the way you experience life.

When your actions are aligned with your intentions, then you will create your world out of those intentions.

Attention is subjective awareness directed to an object. All of us give attention to something in every waking moment of the day.

However, most people don't pay much attention to what they are giving attention to. Their lives are an unconscious stream of thoughts. Life changes when the object of your attention becomes your conscious choice.

Most of your life is directed by habit. Do you have a routine you follow when you get up in the morning? What about when you drive to work or to the store? Have you ever had the experience of driving somewhere you go often and discovering you've arrived without remembering how you got there?

You've driven that route so many times it becomes a habit, while your mind was engrossed in thought (i.e. your attention was on other things). When an activity like driving home has become a habit, all that's necessary is to set the intention to arrive home, and you will end up there.

You can use the fact that we are habitual beings to your advantage. Begin to cultivate success habits.

What are success habits?

- Taking time daily to review your top five passions

- Choosing in favor of your passions whenever you're faced with a decision

- Taking responsibility for the life you've created

- Taking time daily for prayer and/or meditation

- Getting regular exercise

- Getting adequate rest

- Tithing on a regular basis

- Eating healthy foods which support clarity

- Speaking positively and uplifting others through your speech

Research has found it takes twenty-one days to create a new habit. Don't try to do everything at once. Choose one new habit, master it, then move on to another.

What was that mantra we taught you earlier?

What you put your attention on grows stronger in your life.

The second step of manifesting anything is to put attention on its creation. This means developing the habit of giving attention to everything which supports your intention, and being indifferent to those things which do not.

A great teacher once said, "Indifference is the weapon to be used for any negative situation in life."

This means, put your attention on all the good in your life, deal with situations which must be dealt with, and don't dwell on anything which doesn't support what you choose to create.

When Janet found out she needed to put her own plans on hold to look after her stepmother, she could have convinced herself that her dream would never be realized. Had she done that, we probably wouldn't be telling you her amazing story now.

Instead, she focused on what needed to be done in that

moment and it turned out this apparent block in the road was to become a huge gift—in a number of ways.

Unfortunately, most people put their attention on all the reasons their dreams won't come true. Why? Because they're afraid they won't get what they want. If you think some people are just too lazy to pursue their dreams, you'll find that this laziness is a mask for the fear of failure they hold deep inside.

When you are consumed by fear, when your attention is on the things which are going wrong in your life, then in the best case you create inactivity and boredom. In the worst case, you create the things you fear will happen to you.

Yet all of us feel fear from time to time. What do you do when the fear hits?

Facing Fear—The Head-On Approach

If you're like our friend Tellman Knudson of ListCrusade.com, you get excited and push through the fear to the goal.

When Tellman was about 27, he decided he wanted to create a multi-million dollar Internet marketing business. At the time, his office consisted of a makeshift cubicle in his living room, with only a rattling, rusty fan to cool him off in the hot summer, and a CD-ROM drive which he had to take out of the computer and shake in order to play a CD.

One part of Tellman was scared to death, another part of him was completely exhilarated by the challenge. He put his attention on the exhilaration.

He wrote emails to over sixty of the top Internet marketers on the Web. Months went by. Most of them never responded. He kept at it. Eventually a couple of them wrote back and he created relationships with them. After about a year, he connected with Ric Thompson, our partner at *Healthy Wealthy nWise*. He impressed Ric enough to arrange for us to talk. Tellman told us his plan for ListCrusade.com.

He was going to show people how to build a massive email list (one of the critical factors for success on the Internet), while building his own list. He would attract the best of the best on the Internet, along with the best of the best in the personal development arena. His logic was that it's not enough just to learn how to build a list. People also need the personal development skills to live a happy, fulfilled life and be financially successful.

We agreed to help him by connecting with our network of contacts in the personal development arena.

Today, Tellman has over seventy experts who teach both list-building and personal development skills to his subscribers absolutely free. Every week he delivers two interviews to those subscribers, one on personal development, one on list-building. Besides us, the personal development experts include:

- Dr. John Gray (*Men Are From Mars, Women Are From Venus*)

- T. Harv Eker (*Secrets of the Millionaire Mind*)

- Jack Canfield (*Chicken Soup for the Soul*)

- Mark Victor Hansen (*Chicken Soup for the Soul*)

- Robert G. Allen (*Nothing Down, Creating Wealth*)

- Cynthia Kersey (*Unstoppable*)

- Brian Tracy (*Maximum Achievement)*

- Denis Waitley (*The Psychology of Winning*)

The marketing experts include:

- Jay Abraham

- Shawn Casey

- Mark Joyner

- Nitro Marketing

• Joe Vitale

• And many others

In his first three months after launching ListCrusade.com, Tellman had built an email list of over 25,000 and had made over $200,000 in sales. After nine months he had topped $800,000 in sales.

This only happened because Tellman put his attention on what got him excited, not on what scared him.

Facing Fear—The Step by Step Approach

If you're not like Tellman, and you find that fear immobilizes you, then take small steps toward your goal. Each small step achieved will build your confidence and reduce the fear, until you get to the point where you're able to push through the last bit of fear and get on to the result.

With each step, put your attention on what you've already accomplished. Some people find affirmations helpful, like:

"I am capable and successful in achieving my goals."

Personally, we find it more useful when you turn the affirmation into a question:

"What is there about me that could make me successful in achieving my goals?"

The mind is an amazing machine. Ask it a question and it will search for an answer. If you ask a question like this and can't come up with an answer, then find a friend who values and appreciates you. Ask them to tell you the answer. We guarantee they will.

Don't be surprised if they tell you things you didn't even know about yourself, like, you're comfortable to be around, or they feel happier when they spend time with you, or they know they can count on you, or you help them look at things differently.

If you don't see the good in you, it's only because you've gotten into the habit of criticizing yourself. Now is the time to change that habit. Remember what we said about it taking twenty-one days to change a habit?

Post these questions where you can see them each day, and every day for at least 21 days, take a few minutes to write down things you appreciate about yourself. This is so important we have formalized it in our own lives and call it *The Appreciation Game*. We'll share all the details in Chapter 7.

You will find that by putting your attention on your strengths, how capable you are, the reasons you can accomplish your goals, fear will drop away and the results you desire will begin showing up in your life.

No tension means exactly that. Creating intentions and putting your attention on them is a simple, easy, effortless process.

No matter where you are, or what you're going through, you are creating your world by where you put your attention. You don't have to try. You do it naturally.

It doesn't matter whether you're in the midst of a disaster, whether you're a single mother on welfare, or a billionaire real estate tycoon. Every day you create your experience of life from what you give your attention to.

It's a choice. Yet most people don't choose. They unconsciously choose to allow their attention to go to the things they fear the most. And guess what shows up in their lives? That's right. The things they fear the most.

The person caught in the midst of a disaster can choose to focus on the fear of being killed, or on how he can help those around him who need assistance. The single mother on welfare can choose to focus on the fear she won't have enough food for her babies, or she can focus on the things she can do for her babies. The billionaire real estate tycoon can focus on the fear that his fortune will be wiped out, or he can focus on the good he can do with his wealth.

When you become conscious of where you're putting your

attention, it is no more difficult than being unconscious about it. The difference is that now you are aware of what you are creating.

If you want to see how powerful you are, look at your life and what you've created, good or otherwise. It is your creation. Here's the good news, if you're not happy with what you've created, you can begin creating consciously now.

Your passion list and all the other tools we'll share with you in the coming chapters are there to inspire you, excite you, and remind you of what's truly important to you in your life. They are there to help you put your attention on the things that will bring more joy and fulfillment into your life.

If you ever find yourself not wanting to read your passions, or review your goals, or go over your vision, it means you've been straining on these things, or there is an underlying fear that you can't have or achieve what you have written.

When you are truly passionate about something, there is nothing which can keep you from it. You won't have to try to put your attention on it, because it draws you irresistibly to it.

"I tried everything I could think of to get Janet focused on other projects, but nothing could take her attention off her trip to India," Chris will tell you. There wasn't any question about it. From Janet's side, there was no effort involved whatsoever. It was as if this passion drew her inextricably onward of its own volition.

When you write your passions in a way that excites you, when your goals are lofty yet achievable, when your vision is aligned with your heart's deepest purpose, then these things will draw you naturally to them. You will look forward to reading through them. When you feel down, you'll be drawn to reviewing them because they will pick you up again.

When your thoughts are aligned with the deepest stirrings in your heart, then intention, attention and no tension are completely natural and effortless.

YOUR MARKERS

Dr. Naram knew he was passionate about becoming the most renowned Ayurvedic physician and making Ayurveda known throughout the world. With the help of his teacher, he then identified the "Markers" or "Signposts" which would allow him to know he is really living that passion.

From his perspective, these Markers were completely outside the realm of the possible when he wrote them. Yet, he just innocently took his teacher's advice and wrote out the things he'd love to create in his life (his intentions). Then he kept these Markers in mind (in his attention) while he built his Ayurvedic practice. He didn't strain after them. He simply allowed them to show up in their own perfect timing (no tension). And show up they did!

Now, we are giving you that same opportunity. Take a blank piece of paper and write one of your passions at the top of the paper. Then write out 3-5 Markers which will have happened when you are fully living your passion. These are the things which will tell you that your passion is alive and well in your life.

Please don't think about how your Markers will be achieved. Just write them out. Here is an example:

Passion: Being a multimillionaire.

Markers:

1. I earn at least one million dollars per year

2. I have over ten million dollars in savings and investments

3. I travel first class wherever I go

4. I live in my dream home on the ocean with views of the mountains

5. I own a brand-new Lexus sports car

Passion: Being in the moment and trusting my intuition.

Markers:

1. I am fully present with each person I meet and with whom I spend time

2. I experience every day as perfect and the days seem to flow effortlessly

3. I have a clear internal sense about what action is the best for me every moment

4. Others remark on my confidence and how wonderful it is to be around me

Alright, now it's your turn. Create a page for each of your passions and write out your Markers for each of them. Keep these pages because in the next chapter you'll be using them again.

And remember, things frequently don't turn out the way you think they will. Taking care of her stepmother was definitely NOT one of Janet's Markers for spending time with the enlightened. Little did she guess...

6

ALLOWING THE DREAM
TO COME ALIVE

Every moment is a gift,
when we stay open to
what is appearing now.

—*Janet and Chris Attwood*

After hearing that my stepmother needed someone to look after her, I knew this was what I had to do. In a flash I understood why I had hastily packed two large suitcases!

Neither my brother, John, under a lot of pressure with his work, nor my sister, Mickey, in Europe on vacation and not able to be reached, was in a position to look after Margie. I was the only one able to adjust my schedule to stay and care for Margie during her last months.

Staying open to what was appearing moment by moment, I put aside my dreams of being with the enlightened, and moved in with Margie, who had now become my #1 passion.

That was one of the most beautiful times I've ever had. The minute I walked into Margie's house I felt a sense of elation. I was so clear this opportunity to be with Margie in her last days was such a gift. We had been through so much together.

I told her how happy I was that I got to be the one to take care of her and her response brought tears to my eyes.

"Oh Janet, thank you. That makes me so happy. I was so afraid I would be a burden."

The house was overflowing with love.

I was shocked when, after less than a week, Margie's condition deteriorated dramatically. She seemed to be leaving much more quickly than the five or six months the doctor had said she had left.

She had told us many times in recent years she was ready to go. When my Dad passed away a few years ago, she lost the most important person in her life. Now, she seemed to be rushing on to join him.

On the fifth day after I arrived, Margie passed away, quietly and peacefully. Having prepared myself to be in San Diego for many months, I was taken aback by the sudden turn of events.

But there was no time to think about what this meant for my own life. While my sister was overseas, my brother, John, and I dealt with taking care of Margie's body and her estate.

From my spiritual studies, I had been told the importance of honoring a deceased family member for a few days after they die. Before Margie passed away, I asked if I could create a special ceremony for her after her passing.

I told her I had learned from my spiritual teachers that it takes a number of days for the soul to leave the body. To make sure the transition is smooth for the deceased, the friends and family should pray, meditate, sing spiritual songs and read spiritual literature in their presence. Margie loved the idea and said she would be honored if I did those things for her after she died.

When Margie passed away I immediately called a number of funeral homes to see if they would allow me to keep the body at home for three days.

After calling at least fifteen different homes, I finally connected with a woman who had a completely different outlook from all of the others.

When I explained what I wanted to do, this woman said, "How wonderful! Yes, of course, you can keep the body. California law does not require you to move the body immediately. I am from Brazil. There we honor the body of the deceased for a week after a loved one dies."

This great woman told me what to do to preserve Margie's body for the few days it would be at home.

My niece, Tonia, and I bathed Margie and dressed her in her favorite clothes. We collected hundreds of flowers from the neighborhood and then placed them all over her from head to toe, with just her beautiful face beaming out from amongst them. My brother and I gathered all of Margie's plants as well as favorite pictures of those she loved and placed them all around her. Then we lit candles and incense, and created the most celestial environment for her.

During the next day we meditated and prayed, read spiritual literature and played Margie her favorite music. John even insisted on watching the golf tournament and turned the volume up so Margie could hear just in case she was listening. "Golf," John said, "was Margie's favorite sport."

It happened on the second day of her passing that one of my friends who had lived in India for many years emailed me that a great Saint named Bapuji was in Orange County about three hours away and I had to go meet him for my documentary. She didn't know my step mother had just passed away.

When I let her know what was going on, she gave me the phone number to contact one of Bapuji's devotees. My thought was, "Maybe he can tell me if there is anything more I should do for Margie."

I called and got to talk with Prem Avadhoot Bapuji through a translator. After talking with this great Saint for a few minutes, his devotee told me, "Bapuji wants you to know there is a 99% chance he will come tomorrow to bless your stepmother."

I was completely blown away! I excitedly called my brother and said, "You aren't going to believe this one!"

Telling him the story of how I connected with Bapuji, I asked if he might possibly come the next day to give his blessings to Margie.

"Are you kidding, I wouldn't miss it for the world!"

The next day, at the appointed time, a car drove up, and a beautiful, elderly Indian Saint draped in the white traditional Indian clothing called a dhoti got out of the car with his arms full of roses. Those who accompanied him carried a huge basket of fruit.

My passion to spend time with the enlightened was beginning to be realized, in a way I could never have possibly imagined.

Bapuji surveyed the room that Margie was in and smiled. I could tell he was pleased with all we had done for her so far. He carefully handed both my brother and me a rose and had us gently put them across Margie's body. When we were done, Bapuji stood in silence next to Margie for a long time. Then he motioned to my brother and me to sit down on the floor and he proceeded to sit next to us on the couch. He spent the next two hours in silence with us, gently stroking our heads, and showering both of us with love.

When Bapuji was done, he walked to his car, turned to my brother and me and said, "Do you know why I have come?"

"No" I said.

"It was not because of you."

"I didn't think so," I replied.

Then Bapuji looked at us with the most compassionate, loving eyes and, in a gentle voice, said, "I came because when you were telling me about *your step mother I felt such a deep connection that I felt she might have been my mother in a past life."*

With that Bapuji waved good-bye and drove away.

My brother and I just stood there in complete amazement with our mouths hanging wide open!

"This or Something Better"

It was a shock to me when Margie passed. It happened so quickly and unexpectedly.

It was an equally big shock when my brother told me a week later Margie had left a significant estate and I would be receiving a large amount of money very soon.

Suddenly, all the money I needed for my trip to India was available—a gift from my beloved Margie.

♦ ♦ ♦

Janet's experience illustrates one of the most important secrets we have to share with you. When you are clear about WHAT your passions are, you can't predict HOW they will get fulfilled.

OK, we can hear you saying, "That was just a fortunate coincidence. I don't have any rich relatives who are about to die and leave ME a bunch of money!"

This is the point exactly. You can't imagine in advance HOW your passions will get fulfilled. It never occurred to Janet that Margie might pass away and leave her this money. Margie's death was completely unexpected.

Janet couldn't have figured out how she would receive more than enough money to fulfill her passion. What was required of her was to remain open to everything which appeared, without holding on to her own concepts of what she needed.

There are many ways the means of fulfilling your passions can show up. Most of us have been taught that when you want to achieve something, you have to make a plan, execute your plan and then, if you do a good job, you'll enjoy the results.

That well may be exactly how it works for you, and it could also be that in spite of your best laid plans, nothing seems to go the way you expected. In these moments, beware the tendency to think there is only one way your dreams can get fulfilled.

What is required of you is to stay open. Realize that the good in your life may not appear in the ways you think it will. When things happen which are not what you had planned, expected or wanted, let go of your own will and open up to God's will. Watch how your life unfolds and accept what appears now.

When her stepmother needed her, Janet realized her passion to give love and support to her family was more important in that moment than spending time with the enlightened. Yet as it turned out, the love she showered on Margie, was the ground on which an enlightened Saint appeared in her life.

Before we tell you about Janet's unbelievable adventures in India, which came out of the simple process of writing down what she loves the most, let's create your Vision Board, your Passion Pages and write your 100th birthday speech.

YOUR VISION BOARD

Our friend John Assaraf lives near San Diego, California in a gorgeous home on six mountaintop acres surrounded by 320 fruit-bearing orange trees with incredible panoramic views. He is a millionaire many times over from his business successes.

Years ago when John was living in Indiana, he created a Vision Board—a board with pictures of all the things he wanted to create in his life which he had cut out of magazines. One of the pictures on that board was of his dream home.

He put his Vision Board up in his office and kept it there for about a year, as an ongoing reminder of the things he was choosing to create. After that year he put the Vision Board away and never looked at it again.

About ten years later, John and his family had moved to the beautiful home he now owns near San Diego. He was cleaning out the attic one day when he ran across a box with his Vision Boards. He put it aside to toss out as he was going through other things, and his young son said:

"Daddy, what's this?"

"These are boards I made before you were born of all the things I wanted to have some day."

As John pulled out one of the boards to show his son, he was shocked. John looked at the board he was holding and saw the picture he had pasted on it so many years ago was a picture of the very house he and his family were now living in! He had completely forgotten about the board and the specific house he had put on it by the time he went to buy his dream home. Yet, somehow, his mind drew him to the house he had selected as his perfect home.

We tell you this story for two reasons. First, and foremost never underestimate the power of the mind to create the vision you hold. Second, creating a Vision Board is one of the most fun things you can do to begin creating the life of your dreams.

You can get some poster board, or do as Chris did and paste your pictures on a large mirror. The advantage of the latter approach is that it's easy to add and change pictures over time. Janet pasted her pictures in a notebook so she can sit, look at them from time to time and take them with her.

Whichever approach you take, get a big pile of magazines on topics related to your passions and start going through them. Or you can search the Internet to find the pictures you want.

Cut out pictures of the things you want to be, do or have, and paste them on your Vision Board. Put the board somewhere you'll see it daily. You have created a simple set of pictures to remind you of what you choose to create in your life.

Remember that mantra we taught you?

What you put your attention on grows stronger in your life.

A Vision Board is one of the easy ways to keep your attention on the things you really want to grow stronger in your life.

YOUR PASSION PAGES

Was that fun? Of course, if you're like us, you're still reading the book and haven't yet done the Vision Board.

Just remember, the people who are most successful at living passionate lives are the ones who take the time to do their inner homework.

Creating a Vision Board is the kind of thing that's really fun to do with friends. So, if you haven't made your Vision Board yet, throw a vision party and create your board with a bunch of your best buddies.

Let's see, what have we accomplished so far? You have:

• Your top five passions

• Your Passion Cards posted in strategic locations

• Your Markers

• Your Vision Board

Why have you been doing these things?

**When you are clear,
what you want will show up in your life,
and only to the extent you are clear.**

This is what we mean by "inner homework." The cool thing is, this kind of homework is fun!

Are you beginning to get a clearer idea of what your life might look like when you're living your passions? Let's take it to another level and create your Passion Pages.

In Chapter 4 you created a page for each of your top five passions, and wrote down Markers for each one. Now, on that same page write a few paragraphs describing what that passion means to you.

Close your eyes for a minute. Imagine what life is like for you when you are completely living this passion. What does it feel like? How do your days change when you're living this passion fully? Are there any changes to the way you interact with others? What impact does this passion have on your life?

Once you have a clear picture of life when you're living this passion, begin writing.

Do this now.

When you've written a page on each of your top five passions, take a break. When you come back to these sheets in a few minutes, or an hour or tomorrow, read them out loud to yourself.

Begin by reading your five passions. How does that feel? Now read each page you've written on each passion. At the end of each page, stop, close your eyes and picture your life as you've just written it. How does that feel?

Another mantra:

> **My life is created first in my mind,
> then in the world.**

Will your life look exactly as you picture it now? Of course not! It will be better.

The purpose of writing out these pages is not so you can live in some dream world which has no connection to reality. It is to uplift your vision, inspire you, and move your heart to go places you would not have otherwise been able to go.

Your life will always be better than you can imagine it now because you are beginning to consciously create that life. Your future life will be the result of all the evolution and growth you have experienced between now and then.

Your life becomes seemingly "worse" when you are intent on it appearing the way *you* think it should be. When you insist that the world conform to your concepts of what is best, and it doesn't, what happens? You suffer.

Everything in your life is structured for your evolution. The laws of nature which govern every aspect of existence, including our daily lives, are designed to support you in experiencing deeper aspects of your own nature.

When you fight reality, you will lose, and only always. When you realize that every part of your life is working to bring you closer to knowing your true nature more completely, then life can only get better.

When you stay open to how life is appearing at this moment, free of your concepts of how it "should" be, you create the opportunity for miracles to occur.

YOUR 100TH BIRTHDAY

Now we're going to pull all the pieces together into one grand vision of your life.

Today you have the chance to time travel to your 100th birthday, years from now when you are looking back on your whole life.

Imagine it's that day. Your friends and family have come together from all over to be with you. On this day your spouse or your best friend is going to give a speech honoring you for all you have given and shared with those around you over the long course of your life.

And you're going to write that speech now.

What is the legacy you want to create in your life? How do you want people to remember you? Your 100th birthday speech will draw on everything you've done up until now, your passions list, your Markers, your Vision Board, and your Passion Pages, to summarize a life well-lived.

When you write this speech, write it in third person, just as if your best friend or spouse is speaking it out about you, your life, and the influence you've had.

This is your chance to let loose and talk about the kind of life you truly choose to create. Imagine yourself at that birthday party. What will your life look like from that vantage point when you have lived the kind of life you will feel great about?

Who have you loved and who has loved you? What did you create, and what did you teach through your living? Why will people be thankful to have known you?

Your 100th birthday speech will probably be quite a few pages. After all it describes the contribution of your entire life. Here is a short sample of a few of the things Chris might say about Janet on her 100th birthday to help get you started:

♦ ♦ ♦

"Thank you all for coming to beautiful Marin County, California, to this place which Janet has helped make a model of ideal living, to celebrate a life which has affected people everywhere. It's not surprising that there are over 5,000 people here to celebrate the 100th birthday of this beautiful woman who has touched so many hearts.

"Many of you have traveled far distances to be here: from the heights of the Himalayas, to the mountaintops of Nepal, to the great cities of Europe, South America, Australia, New Zealand, Asia, and Africa. Janet's life has been an inspiration for all of us who are committed to living a passionate, fully enlightened life.

"Janet has proven through her own example that miracles happen over and over and over again when we commit ourselves fully to living our passions. Her books, her weekly TV show, her films, her magazines and radio programs have all had one theme: Your passions are the clues to your personal destiny.

"And how appropriate that Janet's life should be dedicated to teaching all of us how to live with passion, when that is what her own life expresses so completely. Passion springs from the heart, and it is the quality of her beautiful, all-encompassing heart which has touched millions and made her TV show the #1 rated show worldwide.

"That same beautiful, loving heart connected with film-goers and won her an Academy Award for her ground-breaking documentary which brought living Saints from around the world into the homes of people in every country.

"Those who know her, affectionately call her Jani Ma, because she has truly been a great mother to all of us, showing us how to discern our personal destinies and live a life of real service.

"Even as she has enjoyed great commercial success, Janet has been an inspiration for her philanthropy. Serving as a role model of a 'reverse tither' she donates 90% of her income each year to causes which raise the quality of life in the world.

"Long after she has left her physical body, Janet's influence will be felt through the work of her foundations, and the billions of dollars they distribute each year to improve lives through health care programs, organic agriculture programs, education programs, financial self-sufficiency programs, community planning programs, scientific research programs, programs for the arts, and programs for uplifting human consciousness.

◆ ◆ ◆

This is a brief sample of a 100th birthday speech. Remember you are unique. Your passions are leading you to express **your** unique gifts. You are you, so your speech will not sound like Janet's or Chris' or anyone else's. It is uniquely yours.

Not everyone's passions will lead to a speech which has such lofty ideals as Janet's, and some could sound more like this:

◆ ◆ ◆

What a delight it is to be here with all those who have been touched by John. John's life has been a life of love.

He loves his family. He loves the ocean. He loves nature. He loves to just meet people at the docks and hang out with them. He can meet anyone and really see who they are. Before they know it they'll be sharing their life's story. John has that unique ability to make everyone feel like they are special and that their life was worth living.

His huge heart flows in all directions. During some of this past century's great disasters, John went into the midst of the devastation handing out $20 bills. He saw that with all the assistance the survivors received, none of it provided the relief of having a few dollars in their pockets.

John is loyal beyond words. Time and time again he has extended himself to help his beautiful wife, Anne, his kids, his sisters, and the friends who fill up his life.

John has always followed his heart. He found a way to merge his love of the ocean with his need for a place to live and for having a source of income. For years he has lived on his boats. His skill in finding old, battered boats with lots of potential has allowed him to create great deals for his customers while still making a great living himself from fixing up the boats he loves so much.

It's so appropriate that John should be surrounded by the family, friends and loved ones to whom he has given so much.

◆ ◆ ◆

Your 100th birthday speech is your chance to express the reason you were put on this earth, to describe how you have, are and will give your gifts to the world. Write it down and see how it makes you feel.

Do it now!

All of the exercises in this book have one purpose in mind: to create clarity about what you would like your life to be.

These tools are not for the purpose of helping you live in a dream world, out of touch with reality. While it appears you are writing about the future, you are not. You are writing down your thoughts, dreams, and vision as they exist in this snapshot of time.

When your 100th birthday comes, we guarantee your life will look differently than you have written it today. What you write is not about the future, because there is no way you can know what the future will be. Your writing today is about your thoughts and feelings NOW.

This process will draw to you more joy, more abundance, more success, more peace, more delight, more of whatever it is you desire. And the specifics of what that looks like when the future becomes today, are part of the mystery of life.

That's why, at the end of each of the things we write or draw, we always put:

This or something better!

As she took The Passion Test™ in 2003, Janet really couldn't have imagined what better meant when she had the thought to "spend time with the enlightened." Boy, was she in for a surprise!

7

THE WORLD IS AS YOU ARE

He who has a why to live for
can bear almost any how.

—Friedrich Nietzsche

With the finances taken care of for my trip to India, it was just a matter of organizing the details. I reconnected with Juliann, who bought all the video equipment we would need.

Then I contacted friends I knew could tell me who are the most enlightened teachers in India and Nepal. Using my natural talent for connecting I got permission to interview a number of these teachers.

When I arrived in India, one of my first stops was a small village in the western part of the country, the home of Prem Avadhoot Bapuji, the Saint who had visited to pay respects to my step mother.

Bapuji invited us to be his personal guests in his home in a remote village outside of Ahmedabad called Linch. Aside from him, there were sixteen family members total. Sons, wives, children, and family friends all lived happily in Bapuji's home.

It was a beautiful home. Simple, but very clean and orderly. Bapuji gave Juliann and me two rooms on the top floor, one to sleep in and the other to meditate in.

My first lesson was not far away.

Our first morning at Bapuji's house, while Juliann was sleeping, I woke up at 4:30 a.m. and decided to meditate. I took a candle into the meditation room, put it on what appeared to be a table top and began my meditation.

After some time, I heard Juliann waking so I went in to say good morning. As we were sitting on the bed laughing at how "normal" we felt in this strange environment with these Indians who couldn't speak very much English, we both started to smell smoke. I looked around and through the door to the meditation room I saw flames enveloping the room.

"Oh my God," I said, "the room is on fire!" My head swirling, I went into action mode. I was always great in emergencies. I immediately remembered that the upstairs bathroom had two buckets of water, as there was no running water anywhere upstairs.

Terrified of burning down Bapuji's house and everyone in it, I screamed at Juliann, "We have to get the water buckets—NOW!" We ran to the bathroom, grabbed the two buckets of water and poured them all over the burning objects in the meditation room as the fire was quickly starting to envelop one wall.

My one and only thought was, "no way am I going to burn down Bapuji's house!"

I ran into our bedroom and grabbed my pillow. With Juliann yelling at me to get out of the burning room or I would die, furiously I fought back the flames, hitting them ferociously with the pillow, hoping for a miracle to occur.

As I was being overtaken by smoke, Juliann, fearing for my life and the lives of everyone in the house, ran out of the room screaming at the top of her lungs, "Fire, Fire!" Not knowing what the word "fire" meant, Bapuji's sons took a while to understand.

As soon as everyone in the house realized what she was screaming about, buckets started arriving from everywhere. In no time, the fire was miraculously put out.

Even before the fire was out, Juliann and I were surrounded by the wives and children and Bapuji, making sure that we were OK. In all the chaos I was acutely aware there was absolutely no concern from anyone for the house, the burned room or whatever belongings had been destroyed.

After making sure Juliann and I had not been hurt, the family members took a quick survey of the damage. One wall and eight very large overstuffed suitcases of the family's belongings were destroyed. I was devastated.

Once Bapuji and the others made sure a second, third and fourth time that Juliann and I were OK, a huge roar of laughter filled the house.

We just stood there dumbstruck. Juliann and I had no idea what they were laughing about.

Bapuji walked up to us and said, "Please don't feel bad, this was a blessing," and walked away smiling. All the other family members smiled in agreement as Juliann and I stood there with our mouths open.

Tears streaming down my face, I looked at Juliann and said, "Who are these people?"

In my humble state, all I could feel was blessed. Blessed to witness what real love in action looks like. I had almost burned down Bapuji's family home in which they had lived forever, and the only comments from them were, "Are you OK?" and quickly following, "It was a blessing!"

◆ ◆ ◆

How can it possibly be a blessing for your belongings to go up in smoke? Bapuji and his family understand that for the new to be created, the old must be destroyed. Because life is constantly evolving, hanging on to the old may prevent the new from coming in.

Bapuji and his family also view all acts of creation and destruction as acts of God, for they believe God is good and God is everything. With this, there can be no thought of being a victim, for they know that all of God's acts are blessings.

This is the same idea which is conveyed in the Bible, "Give thanks in all circumstances, for this is God's will for you." (I Thessalonians 5:18)

On this note Janet's adventures in India and Nepal began. In a little while we'll share why Janet came home saying this was "the best experience of my life," but first we want to give you some tools you'll find helpful on the path to your passionate life.

In coaching thousands of people on The Passion Test™, the one thing we can be sure we'll find when someone is having a hard time believing they could really fulfill their passions is a good ol' case of "low self esteem."

Have you ever noticed when someone is feeling badly about themselves, no matter how much you tell them how beautiful they are, how great they are and how much you love them, they just can't hear it? What follows low self esteem everywhere is the belief "I am not worthy and therefore I can't possibly fulfill my dreams."

Earlier we promised we'd share the secrets we've learned for taking care of the "how" part of fulfilling your passions, once you're clear on the "what." You may remember that Janet began thinking of a number of ways to get herself to India. Yet, looking back we can see that the "how" appeared in ways she could never have figured out on her own. We believe the "how" of living your passions is the result of being aligned with the flow of natural law, with your "higher self."

In this chapter we will share a powerful tool and some fundamental principles we've found essential for connecting with your "higher self," that part of you which is capable of achieving all of your dreams and allowing you to give all of your gifts fully.

THE APPRECIATION GAME (FROM JANET)

For years I suffered from low self esteem. I could go into all of the reasons why, but in the spirit of being proactive, I'd rather share with you one of the tools my friend, Marie Diamond, suggested to me many years ago that truly helped transform the way I saw myself.

Chris and I call it The Appreciation Game.

Every day I would review what I had done that day and somehow find something I appreciated about myself. It didn't matter if it seemed like a small thing. The exercise was to find something I could appreciate about myself, no matter what.

At first this exercise wasn't so easy. I soon started to see how there was a payoff for me every time I allowed myself to feel like a victim. It was interesting what showed up as I looked at why I wasn't appreciating myself and instead chose to feel like I wasn't worthy or capable, or lovable, etc.

I discovered the payoff (and there is always a payoff) of being victimized was that I:

1. *got people's attention*

2. *got their sympathy*

3. *got to give up*

4. *got to not feel worthy*

5. *and the list goes on*

Pretty scary stuff wouldn't you agree?

Finally, after many starts and stops playing The Appreciation Game, I finally kicked my low self esteem addiction and chose instead to put my attention not only on my passions, but also on my achievements.

In my seminars, to illustrate the importance of this point, I share the story Mark Victor Hansen and Bob Allen told me about a study done on two bowling teams.

Bowling team A bowled a game and received a video edited to show only the things they did wrong. The bowlers were told to study the video to improve their game.

Bowling team B bowled a game and received a video edited to show only the bowlers' best performances. They were told to study the video to improve their game.

Both teams bowled again. What were the results? Both teams improved, but improvements in the team which focused on their best performances were far greater.

Got the point? Put your attention on what you do right, on your wins, on the things you do well. You will find your improvement is faster and much greater than trying to fix your mistakes.

Sidebar: Now about this word "mistake"
How about looking at that word once again?
Mis – take.
Are you having an aha moment yet?
Mis – take…as in "Take 1," "Take 2," "Take 3" and so on.
That's right, it's just one "take." You get another chance to do it again! How far out is that? I bet you always thought you were doing it wrong when all along there was just another way which might serve you and all concerned better.
Now that is good!

OK, back to the Appreciation Game. You can play this game on your own or with a partner (it's really fun to play it with a partner who truly loves and appreciates you).

On your own, sit for a few minutes at the end of the day, or first thing in the morning. Make a list of at least ten things you appreciate about yourself, what you've done that day, or wins that showed up in your life that day. Don't repeat any of the things which were on your list the previous days.

Do this every day for a week and see how you're feeling about yourself. You'll get the greatest benefit when you write out your lists.

Not only does writing down your Appreciation Game allow you to actually see all the great things you have done and been, the greatness of you will go in more deeply, and your mind will begin to reverse the self-talk which prevents you from realizing your dreams.

If you are playing the Appreciation Game with a partner, prepare to have some fun. Take turns. You find one thing you appreciate about the other and let them know. Then the other person takes their turn to find something they love about you. Do this ten times.

Now, do another round, except this time, each person says one thing they appreciate about themselves, and you can't repeat anything which has already been said. Notice how you feel after playing the Appreciation Game, about yourself, and about your partner.

THE 7 KEYS TO LIVING LIFE
ALIGNED WITH PASSION

The ability to live life in accord with higher principles is one of the things which distinguishes humans from other animals.

We have discovered there are certain key principles which are essential to living a passionate life. We share them with you here.

1. **Commitment** – Until you are committed, nothing will happen for you. There is nothing more important to creating your passionate life than your unshakable commitment to choosing in favor of your passions. Every day you will be asked to put other things ahead of the things you love most. Keep your passions where you can see them, and learn to say "no" lovingly. Here's one line you can practice:

   a. "I so appreciate your asking, and I'm not able to do that now."

   b. Be sure to use "and" rather than "but." "And" connects you with the other person, while "but" separates.

   c. Vary the words to make them appropriate. Just remember to first appreciate, love, understand, and value the other person, then state what you need.

   d. Lastly, keep in mind point #4 below (Stay Open). What's most important may shift temporarily in the light of urgent circumstances. When Janet found out Margie might not have long to live, her love for her stepmother took precedence over spending time with the enlightened. So be committed, and be prepared to be flexible.

2. **Clarity** – When you are clear, what you want will show up in your life, and only to the extent you are clear. Have you heard that somewhere before? Fuzzy desires give fuzzy results. Use the tools in this book plus any others you find and enjoy to get absolutely clear about what you choose to create in your life. Then realize gaining clarity is not a one-time experience, it's an ongoing process. Take The Passion Test™ at least every six months and review your Markers and Passion Pages at least once a year.

3. **Attention** – What you put your attention on grows stronger in your life. We told you we were going to keep repeating these until they're imbeddjed in your DNA! Pay attention every day, every moment to what you are putting your attention on. You will attract all the people, places and things you need to create those things to which you give attention. As you shift your focus to all the good which is flowing into your life, watch how your life is transformed.

4. **Stay Open** – Your greatest good may not be what you think it is. When you are open to whatever is appearing now, even if it's different than the way you think it should be, you release your individual will and open to God's will for you. This is the path to living your highest purpose in life. This is also the secret to overcoming any obstacle which may arise in your life. When disaster strikes and you are open, you are able to take advantage of the opportunities which inevitably present themselves. By staying open Janet was not only able to enjoy some of the sweetest moments of her life with Margie, she also was able to meet and welcome Bapuji into her home. During times when others are insisting you are going in the wrong direction, remember the words from Robert Frost's famous poem "The Road Not Taken":

I shall be telling this with a sigh
Somewhere ages and ages hence;
Two roads diverged in a wood, and I—
I took the one less traveled by,
And that has made all the difference.

5. **Integrity** – Be as true to yourself as you are to others, and as true to others as you are to yourself. The biggest challenge most of us face is to meet our responsibilities to others while pursuing our passions at the same time. When you make commitments to others, make sure those commitments are aligned with your passions. Once you make commitments, keep them. If something else comes up, talk to the other person and ask their permission to renegotiate your commitment. If they aren't willing or able to make the necessary change, then keep your commitment as you originally made it. Even if it is uncomfortable. Do this a few times and you will become more careful about the commitments you make. And treat yourself with the same respect. When you make a commitment to yourself, treat it in the same way you would treat your commitment to another. That includes being willing to renegotiate your commitment when new circumstances arise. Janet would not have been true to herself if she had ignored Margie's need and just said, "Sorry, I'm committed to spending time with the enlightened so I can't help." In that moment, being with and caring for Margie meant much more to her than spending time with the enlightened. Be true to yourself, and when in doubt, practice principle #7 (Follow Your Heart).

6. **Persistence** – Many begin the journey. Those who finish it are the ones who achieve success and fulfillment in life. In his classic book, *Think and Grow Rich*, Napoleon Hill tells the story of the man who bought property with the intention of mining gold. He discovered what appeared to be a massive vein. He went out and purchased the machinery to mine the gold, but before he made any significant profits, the vein dried up. He dug and dug, then finally, he gave up and sold the property and machinery for a few hundred dollars to a junk dealer.

That dealer consulted an expert who showed him the previous owner had failed because he didn't understand the nature of fault lines. The expert told the new owner he would find the vein again, not far beyond where the digging had previously stopped. The new owner followed this expert advice, and sure enough, found millions of dollars in gold, just three feet beyond where the previous owner had stopped digging.

When you're living life truly aligned with your passions, persistence is not hard. You will find you can't stop, even if you want to. Your deepest passions will drive you, in spite of yourself.

7. **Follow Your Heart** – When all else fails, listen to your heart. Passion emerges from the heart, not from the mind. When you feel confused, or lost, or don't know which direction to head, then just start walking and pay attention to what your heart tells you. Do what you love, follow your heart's direction and the path to fulfillment in life will naturally unfold before you.

IT WAS THE BEST
EXPERIENCE OF MY LIFE

"How was your trip?" Chris asked.

"It was absolutely the best and most amazing experience of my entire life." Janet replied.

"What happened?"

A perplexed expression came over her face.

"I must be flippin' crazy!" she said.

• • •

In spite of all her trials, Janet's trip to India was the best experience of her life.

What made it the best? There was a passion which burned inside her every moment of the day. It didn't matter what was happening on the surface level of life. Sickness, falling off mountains, traveling alone, nothing could shake the love she felt for what she was doing.

This is one of those secrets you want to take special note of:

**When you are aligned
with your deepest,
most important passions,
the ups and downs of daily life
won't be able to throw you off track.**

Here's what it was like in Janet's own words.

◆ ◆ ◆

There is no way to adequately convey the profound experiences and life-transforming events which took place on this trip. But I want you to have a sense of the miracles which are possible when you give yourself over fully to your passions, so let me give you a taste of this remarkable adventure.

After the fire at Bapuji's house, Juliann and I headed for Nepal where my mind would again be blown.

Every step of the journey was magical. First, a friend told us about a 107-year old woman Saint. We went to visit her as she was saying her daily prayers. She paid no attention to us, even after we entered her room, until she had finished her daily ritual.

Then she turned and sang to us of beauty, love and devotion to God. Sitting in this simple hut with this old woman, I felt more comfortable, more at ease, more honored and more privileged than if I had been in the wealthiest palace with the greatest king on earth.

From there I trekked to the top of mountaintops to visit Saints with my guide and camera equipment. I found myself in a hospital room with an Aghori master (Aghori is a tradition which seeks liberation by embracing all things, including things most people in the world consider "bad" or "impure"). Everywhere I went, I was met with love.

You Are Not Your Body

Here's a tiny sampling of what these experiences were like. I had met the Aghori master a year before. He was the master of Dr. Pankaj Naram. Pankaj had told me story after story of the amazing mastery of this man. How he had Pankaj pick out three monkeys from hundreds which were running around, then he repeated a specific mantra and those very same three monkeys came and sat in front of him on the ground.

Pankaj explained that the Aghori was the master of specific sounds which create precise effects in the world, yet the Aghori turned away any who came to learn such things from him. He said that pursuit of powers was a waste of life. "Let man seek realization of the Self and then whatever powers he may want will be his," was his advice.

Pankaj had taken me to visit his Aghori master and explained sadly the Aghori had acquired ear cancer, at the moment he cured a devotee of this terrible disease. I asked Pankaj why this had happened and he said he'd asked the same question of Aghori.

"It is my karma, and my time to pass from this world," was his simple reply.

Now as I returned to Nepal, I visited Aghori in the hospital and was completely melted by the love which met me. I had visited his home, and Pankaj had shown me how the Aghori felt such compassion for all creatures he not only fed hundreds of dogs, cows and other animals, he even put food out for the cockroaches. Now, that's some serious love!

As I left Aghori for the last time in the hospital, I asked him, "Aghori-ji (ji is a term of respect in India), is there anything more which I need to know?"

"You are not your body," he replied. As I traveled throughout India in the following months I thought of this many times as my body was racked with vomiting, diarrhea and intense headaches. Thank goodness I am not my body!

On a deeper level, I understood that Aghori was telling me the reality of my life transcends the physical form of my body. When I let go of the identification with the body, then I open myself to the unbounded awareness of pure Self. This is the domain of bliss, of real fulfillment in life.

Passion leads to fulfillment by helping us to become more intimately connected with our deepest nature. That's why we say your passions are the clues to your personal destiny. Ultimately, your destiny is the spontaneous expression of your pure Self expressed through your individual life.

Staying Open

The path of passion takes some interesting twists and turns. It was about to take a big turn for me.

As it came time to leave Nepal, Juliann came to me and said, "Janet, I can't go, I'm sorry."

"What?!" I screeched.

"I can't go. I need to stay in Nepal and find what my passion is."

Shocked would not even begin to describe my state. Juliann was my producer, the expert who knew how to run the camera, work the microphones and manage the filming. Yet, on some deep level I knew this had to be a blessing. Everything always was.

With just a few hours to go before I had to catch my plane to Delhi, Juliann quickly gave me a crash course in the use of the equipment she had bought for me.

Chris and I wrote a book about staying open in the midst of change called From Sad to Glad. *Now I had the chance to practice. So we said a prayer together and I got on the plane.*

As I traveled from place to place I was told of one great master after another.

Ecstasy

My passion to "spend time with the enlightened" was fulfilled more fully than I could ever have imagined.

A few of these experiences stand out. In Delhi I heard of a great Saint named Hans Baba. He was known for the fact that when he sang, his devotees would enter a trancelike state and have remarkable inner experiences.

I traveled from Vrindavan to Delhi and then back to Vrindavan to be with Hans Baba for about a week.

No one knows where Hans Baba will be at any moment. He goes where the mood strikes him. So, I had to ask around until I found out his current location and then traveled there.

One day when I was with Hans Baba one of his disciples told me today was a Holy day and Hans Baba would be feeding and clothing many Sadhus (holy men) from all over India.

"You should come to the celebration, Janet, there is nothing like it." he said.

Within no time, over 2,000 Indian Sadhus in orange and white dhotis filled Hans Baba's ashram. One by one they were given food, an envelope that contained Indian rupees and a woolen shawl. All a gift from Hans Baba.

After the celebration was over Hans Baba returned to the main hall and again started his melodious trancelike singing.

As he kept up his intonations, one after another, devotees began to rise and dance, apparently in a state of rapture. Later I asked one of the devotees why people are attracted to Hans Baba, and she replied with one word: "Ecstasy."

Ecstasy works for me!

Love Knows No Bounds

I headed south with my friend Martin to the ashram of a great Saint who has become known throughout the world as "The Hugging Saint," Mata Amritananda Mayi, affectionately known as "Amma" or "Ammachi." She got her nickname because she gives hugs to all who come to see her. She's been known to go 24 hours or more, giving her love, through hugs, to thousands of people at a time.

We arrived at Amma's ashram and were immediately led upstairs to greet this amazing woman. Amma's presence is quite remarkable. Her impact is felt in the world through the huge donations her non-profit *organizations have received which are now being used to provide hospitals, orphanages, and all manner of charitable service. After the tsunami which hit southern India and Sri Lanka in 2004, Amma pledged over $23 million dollars in financial aid to build new housing for those displaced, and another one million dollars to support aid efforts for the victims of the Katrina hurricane in the United States.*

In her ashram, Amma is surrounded by thousands of devotees and she rules this place with love, firmness and discipline. Being in her presence is like being in the presence of the Divine. There are no words to describe it.

During my visit, I had the rare opportunity to film Amma as she fed two of her pet elephants. She laughed and played, putting cookies in her mouth as the elephants took them gently from her with their huge trunks.

Ammachi's love seems to have no bounds, and there is nothing which is too lowly for her. At various times she will lead the way in clean up duties, or doing the "menial" labor required to maintain the ashram. She is a living example of humility in action, the personification of love.

I'm told it is very unusual these days to have time with Amma. I felt incredibly fortunate to be able to spend a week at the ashram and observe this great Saint in action.

Treat the Guest as God

I went on to Mysore and after spending a week at the Indus Valley Ayurvedic Center, one of the most sublime, comfortable, luxurious Ayurvedic resorts you can imagine, I spent another week with a Saint who was about as far opposite Hans Baba as one can imagine.

Swami Krishnamurthy is staying here in my house with me in Mill Valley, California for two months as I write these words. I first met him at his 150-acre organic mango farm about two hours outside Bangalore.

Swamiji is a fountainhead of knowledge. Ask him one question and you will receive a complete description of that aspect of life. It seems there is nothing he does not understand in depth.

*I sat mesmerized for hours as he described to me the nature of fulfill-
ment, the experience of Being, the meaning of contact with Source, the
purpose of life, and the ephemeral nature of the things we in the West
call our lives.*

*After his discourses, Swamiji took me out to greet his cows, tour the
mango orchards, pick some grapes and enjoy the beauty of the land in
which he lives.*

*In India, there is an ancient tradition which says one should treat a guest
as God. In Swamiji's home I really discovered what that means. His
family couldn't be more attentive or more giving of their love.*

*There was no need I had which wouldn't be fulfilled, and no comfort
within their ability to provide which they wouldn't offer. It was truly a
remarkable experience.*

Striking the Bull's-eye

*After filming wonderful hours of Swamiji's expositions, I took a flight to
Rishikesh in the Himalayas. I stopped in to visit my old friend, His
Holiness Swami Chidanand Saraswati, affectionately known as Pujya
Swamiji. Pujya Swamiji has millions of followers throughout Asia, and
his good works are unending. Every evening, thousands gather at his
ashram on the banks of the Ganges, overseen by a huge statue of Lord
Shiva, for chanting and Vedic ceremonies.*

*I headed up to Uttar Kashi, high in the mountains of the Himalayas,
known as "the Valley of the Saints." This is a place where many are
drawn who have chosen to retire from the world for spiritual pursuits.
While sitting in a hotel in this tiny town, I had the feeling of being in the
presence of another master.*

*Looking around I saw three Indian men in a corner. I approached them
and asked, "Are one of you by chance a Guru?" Of course, you can
only ask such a thing in the rarified air of the high mountains of the*

Himalayas, but in this environment it seemed quite natural.

One of the men looked very irritated with me, one seemed indifferent, and the third replied, "Madam, you have struck the bull's-eye! This is Pilot Baba (indicating the indifferent man), renowned throughout India."

Later I would discover that Pilot Baba is indeed renowned throughout India and has been filmed as he was submerged in a tank of water for five continuous days. I asked if I could interview him. Pilot Baba smiled and said, "Of course. If it will help the world, why not?!"

As I spent the next few days in the presence of Pilot Baba, he invited me to go with him and some of his devotees to Gomukh, the source of the holy river Ganges which emerges from a glacier, high in the Himalayas.

When the Good is Disguised

Having no clue what I was getting myself into, I immediately said yes. The day we were to begin the long hike, Pilot Baba decided he would not take the trek and asked if I would like to stay in Gangotri with him and a few others. But having heard about the journey to Gomukh, nothing could make me turn back at this point, not even more time with the wonderful Pilot Baba.

"It can be a very rough trip," he warned.

"Are you sure you are up for it?" he asked, concerned.

"Absolutely!" I said. "I do yoga!"

It made no difference to me that it was a seven hour trek through the high mountains. I paid no attention to the fact I only had very thin cotton Punjabis to wear (an Indian dress with cotton pants and a long, dress-like top). The possibility of visiting this very famous pilgrimage spot was too irresistible.

I borrowed a cotton jacket, bought myself a wool cap, a very thin pair of white tennis shoes and socks, joined a group of Pilot Baba's devotees from Japan and off we went.

Now seven hours of walking is a pretty good outing for me under the best of circumstances. But this wasn't just seven hours of walking. This was uphill, in super high altitude and half the time clambering over rocks and huge boulders.

When we left Gangotri the sun was shining with not a cloud in sight.

"A piece of cake," I thought.

Pilot Baba's Japanese contingency snickered as I walked past them in my white cotton Punjabis and clean white tennis shoes.

I'll show them what this Hollywood girl is made of!

About two hours into this hike, it started snowing, and I was beginning to shiver. It was OK as long as we kept moving, but when we stopped to rest, I started shaking all over, my head started to ache, and my stomach was in misery. Worst of all I was becoming totally emotional and started to cry as I was walking.

Almost to Gomukh we stopped at a government camp to rest overnight. Word of my condition spread to other pilgrims at the camp. Not long after I collapsed on a canvas cot in one of the tents, a doctor from Ahmedabad miraculously showed up. He informed me I had altitude sickness. It was nothing to worry about and I just needed to take the pills he left with me.

A little while later a homeopathic doctor arrived who also left me with some remedies. Then an Indian Sadhu (renunciate) came to my tent, gave me a tulsi leaf and told me to slowly chew on it for its medicinal properties. A kind woman dropped in who gave me a pair of her brand new blue jeans so I would be warmer. Someone else brought me a warm pair of mittens and socks, and before long I was well bundled up.

It was the most remarkable experience to be thousands of miles from home and be so well taken care of.

This is another valuable lesson. When you follow the path of your passions, you will find support coming from places you could never have imagined. Your job is to do the best you can with what you have, and be open to all the good that comes to you from those unexpected places.

Be alert. Sometimes the good coming to you may be disguised as something apparently uncomfortable or undesirable, like my altitude sickness. When this happens stay open to see where the good is coming within the discomfort.

In spite of all my extra layers, that night it got so cold I insisted my friend Tapash who was traveling with me, a life-long celibate and meditation teacher from Rishikesh, get in my sleeping bag, not for any conjugal pleasures, but solely for warmth.

I didn't give him a lot of choice as I told him, "Tapash, if you don't get in my sleeping bag I will freeze to death. Get in NOW!"

I can't imagine I would have survived that night otherwise.

The next morning the sun was shining and I felt like a new woman. (Don't you even think that!) As we trekked the final few hours to the source of the Ganges, I was in awe. Tall mountain peaks pierced the sky above, ruling this world with their inherent majesty.

Being in this remarkable setting felt like being in another world. The conveniences of modern life are nonexistent and the stark beauty of the surroundings is breathtaking.

Arriving at Gomukh I joined other pilgrims who came to this place to dip themselves in the frigid waters of the torrent called the Ganges as it emerged from under a giant glacier. Tapash, who had mastered the art of breath control, sat in that water for almost five minutes before I made him get out. For me, it was all I could do to wet myself with this holy, yet absolutely freezing water.

My predominant memory of this time is deep-felt emotions which rose to the surface. The profound spiritual quality of this place brought tears to my eyes. I wish I could find words to describe it, and it was one of those indescribable moments. To know what I'm talking about, I think you'll just have to come with me next time (bet you're looking forward to that! ☺)

As I climbed over rocks to get a better shot of the emerging Ganges, all of a sudden, my foot slipped, and down I fell, tumbling over the boulders only to stop within a foot of the raging waters of the Ganges. Had my fall not been broken at that point, you wouldn't be reading this story right now. It was definitely one of those near-death moments.

With reticence, I left this mountain cathedral and back at the tent camp found a donkey to carry me the rest of the way home. I fed my donkey some of the treats I had with me, then as I walked around to his other side, he gave me a belting kick! Down on the ground I went. Fortunately, no serious damage was done.

Beauty Beyond Description

I returned to Uttar Kashi and stayed for a few days at a gorgeous little guest house to recover. I can't begin to describe how sublime this time was. I spent my days by the side of the Ganges, surrounded by mammoth mountains covered with trees, under a clear blue sky. Spending time in deep meditation I understood why the Holy men chose the Himalayas to realize the Divine. Here it was so effortless.

While I was hiking around the Himalayas I heard of a revered Saint from England who lived in a small hut by the banks of the river. Just hearing about her purity and love I knew I had to find her.

Nani Ma has spent over thirty years in India. During her time in the Himalayas she spent many months at Gomukh where I had just been, dipping herself in the freezing waters of the Ganges three times a day as a spiritual purification.

After much coaxing, she finally allowed me to interview her. Now, I wasn't sure how this would work, as Nani Ma is not a particularly *attractive woman. She was in an auto accident as a child and one eye is half an inch above the other, she hasn't had any dental work for years so her teeth appear to be in dire need of attention, and she has hardly any hair.*

However, once she began to speak I started to understand what real beauty is. This remarkable woman spoke with such depth of understanding and her beautiful heart overflowed so completely, that Nani Ma transformed into a beautiful goddess right before my eyes.

With tears streaming down my face, I could hardly hold the camera. Never had I seen someone so completely transformed.

"Nani Ma," I said crying. "Thank you so much. You have truly shown me what "real beauty" is.

Once again I understood why spending time with the enlightened is such a passion for me. This woman is like none I have ever met. She has such a profound understanding of life, her words were so simple, yet so illuminating, and she is a living embodiment of love.

Very few people know Nani Ma is present in the world, and yet I have no doubt her silent inward quality of life has as profound an effect on some level as the great boundless activity of Saints like Ammachi, or Pujya Swamiji.

Miracles Come in Many Forms

I traveled back to Rishikesh and went to visit my dear friend, a beautiful woman Saint, Devi Vanamali. She and Nani Ma share the same deep inner beauty.

Vanamali welcomed me into her home. I sat for hours transfixed by her profound insights and wisdom. One morning before I was leaving, she told me there was a remarkable healer in Kerala named Sri Sunil Das whom I absolutely had to go see.

This man had been diagnosed with terminal cancer about five years before and had been cured of the disease by Sai Baba (another revered teacher with millions of followers in southern India). With Sunil Das' cure came the ability to cure others and he had been using this special gift ever since.

Vanamali told me that Sunilji feeds over 5,000 local villagers every day, treats more than 35 leper families daily and leaders from throughout India come to his simple home for healing.

Now, under other circumstances I would have been thrilled. But I had already been in India for over three months, and Kerala was in the far south of India, a long trip from Vanamali's home in the Himalayas near Rishikesh.

I put the thought aside and went back to Rishikesh to prepare to return to Delhi the following day.

While I was eating breakfast, Devi Vanamali's cousin Mohan came to say good bye to me.

"I have a message from Sri Sunil Das," Mohan said excitedly.

"Sri Sunil who?" I asked.

"Sri Sunil Das. The healer that Vanamali told you about yesterday."

"Oh," I said. Unimpressed, I kept chewing my toast and looking out the restaurant window at the beautiful Ganges river below.

"He gave me a message for you," Mohan said.

"Uh huh," as I buttered my sixth piece of toast.

"He said to tell you that you have great blessings from three Himalayan masters."

He finally got my attention.

"Maharishi, Yogananda and Babaji," Mohan exclaimed.

Upon hearing those three names I immediately dropped my toast in my lap.

"Who?!" I asked in disbelief.

"Maharishi, Yogananda and Babaji," Mohan repeated, smiling.

My heart felt like it had stopped beating. Maharishi Mahesh Yogi is my master with whom I have studied for over thirty-six years, Yogananda was the first master I had ever known and Babaji had lived in my heart ever since I read about him in Yogananda's Autobiography of a Yogi.

"Can we call Sunil Das?" I asked.

"Of course!" Mohan said as he grabbed my cell phone, dialed the number and handed me the phone.

"Hello?"

"Codi, codi pranam," a voice said. "You come?"

When I heard that voice I knew there just wasn't an option, so I said yes, I would come. A few days later I arrived at Sunilji's home near Coimbatore in Kerala and was welcomed with open arms.

This man in his early forties struck me with his down-to-earth, playful, fun, and apparently "normal" personality. Yet his humility, innocence and the profound effect on everyone who meets him are undeniable.

I watched as every day thousands of villagers from throughout that area came and were fed from Sunilji's kitchen. I filmed the faces and deformed bodies of lepers who had suffered from this dread disease for years, in some cases for more than forty years, and who now smiled and laughed.

I sat day after day as people from throughout India came to Sunilji with one ailment or another and received his prayers, his blessings and the healing which he insists comes from God.

I heard story after story of the miraculous which seems to follow Sunilji wherever he goes, and I witnessed many, many cases when he manifested sacred ash and gave it to those who visit him to treat their diseases. From statuettes to pearls, to pendants to bells, Sunilji was constantly materializing gifts out of thin air.

I can't imagine that these feats were concocted after having watched them so many times, and yet these are not the things which make Sunilji special. That comes from his deep devotion to God. Every moment of his day is committed to service, in the name of God. Every "healing" his visitors experience he credits to God.

He takes no money for himself. All donations go to the charitable trust established to support his work which is run by the former President of India.

Sunilji showed me what a life of service truly looks like and it is an amazing thing to witness.

After I had stayed in his home for some time, I learned that my friend, Jack Canfield, was coming to Bombay. I immediately had the thought, "What can I do to make Jack's visit to India extra special?"

I made some arrangements and then flew to Bombay to meet Jack when he arrived. I met him at his hotel and discovered Jack's bags had never arrived from the U.S. So, we spent our first few hours together in one of my favorite activities—shopping!

It turned out Pujya Swamiji and Sadhvi Bhagwati Saraswati from Rishikesh were in Bombay at that time, as were my friends Catherine Oxenberg (well-known actress and princess of Yugoslavia) and her actor husband Casper van Dien (Starship Troopers, Sleepy Hollow, The Omega Code, Tarzan, and others). I made arrangements with Pankaj and Smita Naram for us all to have dinner together the night before Jack's seminar.

Was that an amazing evening?! Imagine having dinner with two Saints, one of the best-selling authors in the world, two world-famous Ayurvedic physicians, and two famous movie actors. It was definitely one of those memorable moments.

I spent the next few days with Catherine and Casper in their suite at one of Bombay's finest hotels. During those days it happened that Sunilji was also in Bombay, asked to come by one of his famous devotees.

I took Sunilji to the airport as he was leaving Bombay and got a call from a dear Indian friend who is very well-respected in that city, sitting on the boards of more than twenty-five educational institutions. I had introduced her to Sri Sunil Das the day before. One of her oldest and dearest friends was in the hospital and appeared to be dying. She was deeply distressed and asked if Sunilji could come.

"Oh Maya, I'm so sorry. Sunil Das just got a call from the royal family in Kerala and they need him to come right now. I'm so sorry," I told her.

As I hung up the phone, Sunil Das said, "Janet go!"

"Huh?!" I stammered.

"You go!" he said.

"Sunilji, what can I do?! I'm not a healer!" I said.

With those words, Sunil Das immediately manifested from thin air the grey ash known as vibhuti, or healing ash.

Handing the ash to me, Sunil Das said, "You must go immediately, do not stop, go immediately." He then instructed me to put the sacred ash into the dying woman's mouth.

With that, off I went. Although I was sorely tempted to stop along the way at some of the great shops I had planned to be visiting that day, Sunilji clearly told me to go immediately, so on I went.

When I walked into the room I was surprised to find a young girl sitting on the bed of the dying woman with her head on the woman's stomach. The girl immediately looked up at me and said, "Oh Janet, I'm so glad you are here! My mother is dying."

These words came from Premala, another of my dear Indian friends. As it turned out it was Premala's mother who was dying (a fact I didn't know until that moment).

I took Premala's hand and began singing the Mrityunjaya mantra, a special chant I had been taught for those who are sick or dying or in need of protection. Within a few minutes of my arrival, Premala's mother took three deep breaths and passed away.

Aware of a beautiful light that was flooding the room, I said to my friend who was now sobbing uncontrollably, "Premala, can you feel how happy your mother is?" With those words Premala stopped crying. "Can you feel how light it is in the room, Premala?" I asked.

"I can," she said, as her eyes grew wide with wonder.

"I can!" she said again, and started smiling and laughing all at the same time.

Later Premala told me my coming to the hospital had been a true life saver for her. After my arrival and taking the sacred ash from Sunilji, she felt her mother had been truly blessed. The deep grief she had been feeling lifted and she felt a great relief.

This is one of several experiences which caused my respect for Sunilji to deepen to a profound level. Somehow, he had known it was urgent that I go immediately to the hospital and as a result, a profound effect occurred.

When Your Passions Start Coming to You

I have been back from India for several months now. After spending months traveling throughout India and Nepal meeting the most remarkable individuals I have ever encountered, my passion to spend time with the enlightened continues to be fulfilled, over and over again.

Since returning home, my Saintly friends have been coming to me. A few weeks after my return, Hari Prasad Swamiji, a master whose birthday I'd attended, along with 80,000 other people, came to my home to visit. A few days later, five of his female renunciates called "Benus" came and stayed for several days, filling my house with laughter and love. Then not long after, my dear Bapuji came for a couple of days, and the profound Swami Krishnamurthy, at whose home I had been treated with such kindness, is now here for two months.

My life has become a series of miracles. In my upcoming book, The Saints Speak Out, I'll share all the details of this remarkable trip, but hopefully you have a taste of why I called this the best experience of my life.

Trekking to the source of the Ganges, discovering that fire can be a blessing, witnessing the effects of Sunilji's apparently miraculous healings, listening to Swami Krishnamurthy's profound discourses, these experiences were amazing. Then, experiencing the divine love in the presence of Ammachi, Bapuji, Hans Baba, Hari Prasad Swamiji, Nani Ma, Devi Vanamali, and all of the other Saints I was blessed to meet completely blew me away. Add to that all the other remarkable events on this incredible journey. This is what made my trip to India the most transforming experience of my life. And those experiences weren't the whole of it.

It was also the best and most amazing experience because I learned what is truly possible when you allow yourself to give in fully to going for what you love. I learned that money will show up when and as it is needed. I learned how important it is to let go of one's own concepts of how one's passions will get fulfilled and stay open to how life is appearing. I learned that the obstacles and challenges along the way simply don't matter when you feel the fire of passion inside—with that fire nothing can stop you.

Perhaps most importantly, I learned once again, that God is good and God is everything. When I am willing to let go of my will and open to God's will, meaning the way life is unfolding, then life becomes an incredible adventure and consistently fulfilling.

◆ ◆ ◆

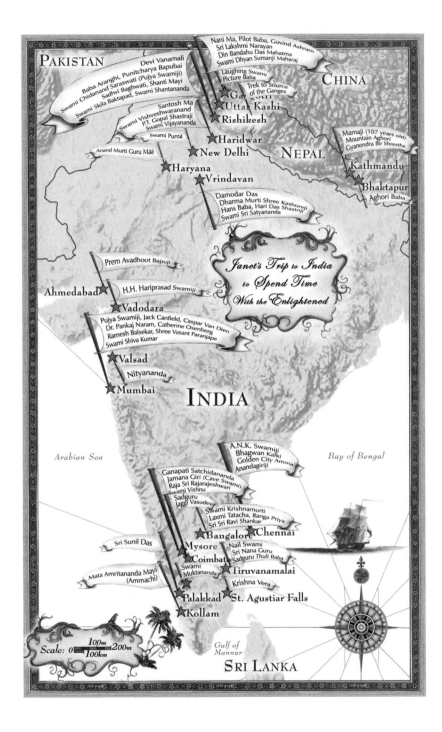

THE POWER OF PASSION

Passion has the power to transform your life. When you discover your deepest passions, you connect with the essence of who you are. When you live life aligned with your passions, your personal destiny unfolds naturally and effortlessly.

When that happens, life becomes an expanding field of joy, happiness and fulfillment, along with all the same inconveniences, challenges, obstacles, and discomforts everyone experiences. The difference is, on the path of passion, those things just don't have much significance.

In the previous pages we've given you tools to create greater and greater clarity about your passions, and the things which are most meaningful to you. Have we told you enough times how important clarity is to create the life of your dreams?

Now that you have the tools, we are going to share with you the experiences, wisdom and sage advice of those masters of transformation in the West who have been extraordinarily successful at living passionate lives.

Benjamin Franklin had this to say about gaining wisdom:

"There are two ways to acquire wisdom;
you can either buy it or borrow it.
By buying it, you pay full price in terms of
time and cost to learn the lessons you need to learn.
By borrowing it, you go to those men and women who
have already paid the price to learn the lessons
and get their wisdom from them."

When you borrow the wisdom of those who have already paid the price, you can shortcut the path to fulfilling your own destiny.

In the second half of this book, we will introduce you to some of the most remarkable people in the Western world, so you can borrow their wisdom for living a passionate life. This is just a sampling of the amazing interviews from the Passion Series, the cover story interviews we conduct monthly for *Healthy Wealthy nWise*.

You are invited to be part of the live teleaudience for these incredible calls as our guest. All you need to do is register by going to:

http://www.healthywealthynwise.com/interview

If you were inspired by Janet's stories of her meetings with some of the Saints of India and Nepal, then you may also want to join us for our Dialogues with the Masters calls. Once a month we connect with one of these enlightened individuals by teleconference and ask them questions submitted in advance by the participants.

When you register for the Passions series, you will receive an invitation to register for the Dialogues calls as well. There is no charge to listen to the live calls for either the Dialogues with the Masters, or the Passion series.

Special Note: If you aren't going to read the interviews in Part 2 right away, then be sure to go now to the Epilogue on page 203. There you can review the key lessons we've discussed in the book.

Part Two

THE PASSIONS OF REAL LIFE LEGENDS

You are only as powerful as your mentors.
—*Mark Victor Hansen and Robert G. Allen*

Successful people have mentors—teachers who have helped them find the shortest route to their goals, overcome obstacles along the way, and stay inspired and motivated on the path.

Every month we interview people at the top of their fields about what it took for them to get aligned with their passions.

These interviews are phenomenal. There is nothing like hearing people who are so clearly successful in living passionate lives. To learn how to get aligned with your passions, the most valuable thing you can do is listen to people who already are.

Our interviews have included people like:

• Stephen R. Covey, *The 7 Habits of Highly Effective People*

• David Lynch, award winning director of *The Elephant Man, Blue Velvet, Mulholland Drive,* and *Twin Peaks*

• Jim Rohn, multimillionaire mentor

• T. Harv Eker, *Secrets of the Millionaire Mind*

• Neale Donald Walsch, *Conversations with God*

With permission of *Healthy Wealthy and Wise* magazine we have included edited versions of six of these interviews here so you can learn from some of the most accomplished people in the world. The full recorded interviews along with transcripts are available to members of the magazine's Real Life Legends Club at:

www.healthywealthynwise.com/rllclub

8

RICHARD PAUL EVANS

FAILURE IS NOT AN OPTION

By: Janet Attwood

*When **Richard Paul Evans** wrote the #1 New York Times best seller, The Christmas Box, he never intended on becoming an internationally known author. Officially, he was an advertising executive, an award-winning clay animator for the American and Japanese markets, a candidate for State Legislature and most importantly, a husband and father.*

His quiet story of parental love and the true meaning of Christmas made history when his self-published book became simultaneously the number one hardcover and paperback book in the nation. Since then, more than eight million copies of The Christmas Box have been printed.

During the Spring of 1997, Richard's Christmas Box Foundation started the idea for The Christmas Box House, a shelter for abused and neglected children. An acclaimed speaker, Richard has shared the podium with such notable personalities as President George W. Bush, President George and Barbara Bush, former British Prime Minister John Majors, Ron Howard, Elizabeth Dole, Deepak Chopra, Steve Allen, Bob Hope and more.

He's been featured on The Today Show *and* Entertainment Tonight, *as well as in* Time, Newsweek, People, *the* New York Times, Washington Post, Good Housekeeping, USA Today, TV Guide, Reader's Digest, *and* Family Circle *and on the cover of* Healthy Wealthy nWise.

His latest book is called Five Lessons a Millionaire Taught Me.

Janet: Richard, in this series, we're particularly interested in examining how following one's passions, the things you love the most, contribute to a person's success. Will you tell everyone how the things you loved the most led to your writing *The Christmas Box?*

Richard: When I first wrote *The Christmas Box,* I felt this tremendous love for my children and it was something brand new in a way.

I didn't necessarily want to have children, and when I made that decision, I didn't know how it would affect my life. It opened up so many doors and changed my life in so many ways, that when I wrote *The Christmas Box,* I wanted to somehow capture that. I wanted to share with people the joy that comes from the service of raising children.

Janet: I was reading something saying you had written it as an expression of love for your two daughters?

Richard: Exactly. That's exactly what it was. It wasn't a book that was to be published or to spread around the world. I wanted to capture that feeling, so that someday, when they held their own child in their arms, they could then think of and understand how

I felt about them, as a father. Initially, my whole idea was to make two copies of the book.

Janet: So you never had an idea you would publish this book?

Richard: No. Outside of making a little copy to put under the Christmas tree, that was it.

Janet: So what happened?

Richard: When I finished the book I was so moved by the experience I wanted to share it with people, so I gave a copy to my wife, Keri, and she too was moved by it. I started to share it with family and friends and decided rather than doing two copies, I was going to do twenty copies. We were going to do them as Christmas presents, so that's what we did.

I went out, made twenty copies and handed them out as Christmas presents, and that's where it all started.

Janet: Now I heard that from those twenty copies being spread around, bookstores started calling you. Is that true?

Richard: Exactly. I was receiving phone calls almost every single day from people reading the book. About six weeks after I gave those books out as Christmas presents, I received a phone call from a local bookstore.

The clerk just said, "Hello, Mr. Evans. Did you write a Christmas story?"

I said, "Yes."

She said, "Oh, good. Where can we order it?"

"You can't order it. The book's never been published."

She said, "Well, I've had ten orders for that book this week."

Janet: Oh my gosh! That is a miracle. That's what I call support of nature. When you're so aligned with what you're supposed to be doing, that nature just takes over and opens all the doors.

Richard: Exactly. I've always maintained this book had its own life and its own mission, and I felt more dragged along with it. I would give the book enough to do what it needed to do to get to the next level, and then it would take off.

Janet: This leads me to my next question because many of our readers are aspiring authors themselves. Would you share some of the secrets which allowed your book to become a number one *New York Times* best seller?

Richard: Absolutely. The first thing to remember that's most important about the book is that it was *the book*. I remember when someone said, "It's the economy, stupid." And it's like, "It's the book, stupid." The book was special. Even though I've become a more savvy marketer, I have not been able to duplicate the success of *The Christmas Box* since. None of my books, even though they've all been *New York Times* best sellers, have sold at that level.

When I started, the first thing I realized was that because I was passionate about it, I actually had an advantage in being self-published. When you work with a larger publisher, it's a business. They're good at what they do, but they're going to put out more than 100 different books.

So they throw a book out there. If it doesn't work right off, then they'll probably drop it. As a self-published book, I cared a lot about it. I was willing to go to bat for the book. This was after I saw the book was indeed, powerful. I had the belief of destiny with the book. I had a belief that if people just read it, then they would change, and that's what I found.

I remember the first time I met Jack Canfield and Mark Victor Hansen. I was at my very first book show. *Chicken Soup for the Soul* was just taking off, and I know Jack still talks about this in his seminars today. He remembers the first time he saw me, I'm standing next to a mountain of books.

My idea was, "I'm going to go there, give away 5,000 copies of my book, because I believe that if 5,000 people read my book, they would take it out and spread it, and it would become a number one best seller." The first thing was to get the book into people's hands and let them read it.

I started to practice what I call "guerrilla marketing." I know there's now a book about that, but I was calling it that before the book. It's like, "Okay, if I can't win the big war against the big publishers, how *can* I win?" Well, I can be, if not a big fish, at least a medium-sized fish in a small pond. I can win in the little markets.

I would go to little cities no one cared about and get on the radio. They were looking for something to talk about, I could tell them about my book, and I began to learn what people were connecting with in the book. I learned why they liked the book and what affected them and why they wanted to share it.

As I learned those things, I got to the point where I would go on these radio interviews and my distributor could actually track me around the country because every time I would go on a radio interview, they would get four or five calls from bookstores in that city, looking for the book.

I learned how to talk about my book.

I don't know if you've studied the life of Ronald Reagan at all, but in the early days, he signed a contract with, I believe it was General Motors.

He hated to speak, and he wasn't very good at it. People would walk out on him. What happened was, because he did so much of it, he decided, "I'm going to get good at this," he started to work very hard at getting good at it, and he came to be known, throughout history, as "the great communicator."

My first interviews for *The Christmas Box* weren't very good. They weren't interviews on radio—I was talking to people at book signings. People would come up and say, "What is this?" At first, if I'd tell people, they'd walk away. They weren't that interested.

Then one day, I came across something that made them say, "Oh, that sounds interesting. I'll buy the book." I was learning, and so I would find another thing. What I learned near the end was, more than half the time, if someone talked to me, they would buy the book. So I learned what sold the book. I learned how to speak about it, and I was able to talk from a level of passion.

If I didn't care about the book, it never would have happened, but they saw that passion coming through me, and they wanted to share that, so they would buy the book. Then, after they would buy the book, they would read it and they'd come back to buy more, because they wanted to share the message.

So the growth of the book was exponential, but it really was a sense of guerrilla marketing. I started in little cities, I got it out wherever I could, and what was interesting was that the book was a best seller in grass roots America before it hit the *New York Times*. In fact, it was growing so quickly, that all of a sudden this book without a publisher shows up at number two. From nowhere to number two in the *New York Times*. It stunned everyone. At that point, my whole world exploded. I was getting calls and movie offers—from Spielberg's company to the top publishing houses in the world.

Janet: Richard, one of the things I'm hearing, listening to you, is you were so passionate about the book you went out and started doing things even though you didn't necessarily know what to do or what to say in the beginning.

Richard: I knew nothing. I knew nothing about the industry. In fact, I think any time you're following your passion, you're going to be tested. Not to confuse things with your Passion Test, Janet, but there are things that test how much we really care about something.

I was at the Mountains and Plains Book Show in Colorado. I didn't have a lot of money. I took all the money I had and put it towards marketing. I went to this book show and I'm there, handing out copies of my book, meeting bookstore owners. What we found at the show, was that no one was coming through the main area where the booths were.

Here I had spent a sizeable portion of my very meager budget to be at the show and I was frustrated, so finally I went up and asked someone who was walking through, "Where is everyone? There are thousands of people here. How come there's no one in the hall?"

He said, "Well, because they're out with the authors." I walked out, and sure enough, what had happened—the publishers would bring in some of the top authors in America and they would give away free books, so these bookstore owners would stand in line and walk through these lines, get all these books for free, autographed.

Then they'd go, get back in line, and wait for the next slug of authors to come through. So I'm sitting out there watching this happen and watching my dreams vanish, because I'm a nobody. No one cares I'm at the show. No one knows who I am, and here are famous authors.

So I'm sitting there watching. All of a sudden, I had this thought. I looked up at the table and there was an empty seat. I thought, "What is stopping me, besides security and the people at the show, from just walking up there and sitting with the authors?"

I looked at it, and I'm shy. I thought, there is no way. I turned around and started to walk away. I had brought my books with me, because I thought maybe I could go hand them in the line, and I started to walk away and it just hit me. "How much do you care about this book?" That was one of those gut honest moments when it's like, "Well, I care a lot."

Then, "If you don't do it, who will?" I bit my tongue, and I turned around and I'm doing it. I can't believe I'm doing this, and I walked up around the back. I came through the curtain and sat down between two best-selling authors. I sat down at this table, absolutely terrified.

The worst thing that could happen then… one of the organizers, of course, immediately spotted me. The woman walks over to me, and right when she gets to me, I looked up and I said, "Sorry I'm late." The woman was stunned.

She looked at me for a moment, blinked, and she said, "May I get you some water?"

I said, "Sure." I sat there and finished out this whole long line of people coming through, sitting next to best-selling authors, signing my books, and accomplished what I needed to accomplish. The next year, I came back as the number one best-selling author in the country. I was the featured author at the entire show. People were in line to see me.

Janet: Was the woman who gave you the water…

Richard: She was there. She's been there every year. I walked up and said, "Do you remember me, per chance?"

She smiled and said, "Yes, I do. Good for you."

I said, "Thank you for not throwing me out."

She said, "Honestly, I was going to. That's my job. I was walking over to tell you to leave. When you looked up and I saw the earnestness in your eyes, I thought, 'What is it going to hurt? Now here is someone chasing his dream, as crazy as he may be. It's not going to hurt anyone to let him sit here and give away his book.'"

So she got me water instead of throwing me out, and look how it came back to bless both of us. That, to me, was one of those gut check moments when I asked, did I really have passion? When people say, "You're so lucky," it's like, no, you have no idea. I was willing to fight for this book. I was willing to do uncomfortable things. I was willing to take chances. I was willing to risk everything for this book.

When you have that kind of passion, fate just favors the bold.

All of a sudden, things will just start. You will struggle and you'll fight, but you will win.

Janet: This was your passion, and I hear you were shy and put yourself out there. Were there any other obstacles that you experienced along the way, and how did you overcome them?

Richard: Well, this is important to understand, and if you remember nothing else from our discussion here, remember this. We do not succeed in spite of our obstacles and challenges. We succeed precisely because of them.

I want to repeat that.

"We do not succeed in spite of our obstacles and challenges. We succeed precisely because of them."

I had a discussion with the woman who edited *The Christmas Box*. She said, "I've watched you over the last three years, and it's amazing—everything you did seemed to hit an obstacle and failed." She said, "I don't know how this happened. It's like your book was built on failure."

I said, "It was. I was turned down by every publisher I took it to. I was turned down by the distributors. When I got into the national market, I was turned down by all the TV people." It's like everything went wrong over and over and over.

It's what had to happen, because when it finally got to that level where it could take off, the story wasn't, "What is *The Christmas Box* about?" The press did not care about that.

What the *Today Show*, and what *Time* magazine, *Newsweek*, the *New York Times*, and the *Wall Street Journal* were talking about was this guy who was rejected from every publisher he went to. He had no publisher, he had no experience, and he beat the publishing world. That's what became the media story.

That's what fueled it into the hyperselling levels it hit. The failures and obstacles I went through were precisely what I need-ed. They gave me the ability to succeed. I hit obstacles every day. I felt like every time I did something, it failed.

It seemed like it was a constant humiliation. When it hit the level of success, I just thought, "This is amazing. What an amazing lesson about life."

Janet: I am so thankful to you for sharing this story. What I got from it was number one, you had to have the love. You had to have the passion so you could completely go to bat and full-tilt boogie, believe in the destiny of it, and have the belief in the people that they'd read it.

You went out, bought the 5,000 books and handed them out. Then I heard you say that from doing all the radio shows in all these little cities, you started to hear what they needed and what they wanted to know.

Tell me about Christmas Box Houses International. How did the houses come about and what are your plans for them?

Richard: The Christmas Box House is probably what I would call my latest passion. It's a thing that keeps me up at night think-ing about it, and the size of it, to me, is daunting. After *The Christmas Box* took off, my wife Keri and I were concerned about how the money might affect our family; that having a lot of money might negatively affect our children, which would be horrible irony, since the book was written for our children.

So we decided we would teach our children how to use the money to make a better world. We decided, not knowing anything about child advocacy, that we would find out what abused chil-dren needed most, how we could help them. We just started ask-ing questions. We ended up at the University of Utah Graduate School of Social Work.

We asked the Dean, "What's the most important thing we

can do for these kids?" We focused everything on the one question, "What is the most important thing we can do to help these abused children?"

His answer was, "I don't know."

"Well, if you don't know, who knows?"

He said, "Well, let's invite everyone who knows anything about it and let's hold a conference."

We got together in the conference and we learned three things. First of all, these people didn't like each other and they were competing for the same funds, so they saw each other as competition. Second, they didn't communicate with each other because of that. And third, they all agreed on what needed to happen. That's where the concept of The Christmas Box House was born.

We created this facility, it's very large. The first facility was $2.7 million. We learned a lot from it. We made every mistake possible. It grew from there. We got smarter with all of our mistakes. By the time we built our last facility, we built it for less than half the cost.

It's just as effective, and we have housed more than 15,000 abused children since we opened. We are now moving into other countries and we are getting calls from all around the world from people to help them establish Christmas Box Houses in their area.

My greatest passion right now, tied in with this concept, is that I have this dream of creating an army of child advocates, an army 50,000 strong. I believe we can create an army with 50,000 people who care about children, want to stop abuse and help these children in need.

So we did a test and started what we called The Christmas Box Club, and we did the first one in Salt Lake City. It grew too fast so we had to abandon the project, because it was growing so fast, we weren't ready for it. That was two years ago.

We studied it, we plotted better and we just started them

again, and again. Now they're growing very quickly. We are about to open our third club and eventually we expect to have hundreds of clubs around America with tens of thousands of members who are going to help these children in their community.

Janet: You know, in *The Passion Test*™, I say we don't have to know how our passions are going to get fulfilled, we just have to get absolutely clear on what they are and be totally committed to their fulfillment. I think you believe that, is that true?

Richard: I'm very clear on what I want. I want an army of 50,000 people, and I have had a vision of it already. I know the day will come when I will come out on stage, look out over this huge auditorium and see child advocates from around the world. We are going to be one and we're going to change the world.

Janet: Even though you have the passion, the love, the commitment, with all these obstacles, even now, would you say that fear shows up? Even with all you've gone through?

Richard: Always. Yes, it can, it does, but you have to realize fear is the opposite of faith. Fear is something you recognize for what it is, and it can be empowering, but you don't let it linger. You can't have fear and faith at the same time in your mind, because faith is simply a state of mind.

Fear can help you recognize reality and that's a service and that's a good thing. But then when you're ready to move, then you don't take counsel from fear, you let it go. It's like, OK, I'm going to overcome that. I believe I can do this.

Janet: Right, there are no mistakes, there are no failures. I mean, those greatest lessons are the ones that build in us that invincibility, that inner strength. There's nothing lost only everything gained. Thank you for that.

Richard: I was in a meeting once for The Christmas Box

House where everything had gone wrong. We were more than a million and a half dollars in debt. I had totally tapped out any money I could get. I mortgaged everything I owned. I mean financially it put me in jeopardy.

My dad, who was one of four of us working on this project, said to me, "Rick, it's over. The ship's going down. It's time to jump ship."

I said, "No, dad. If this ship goes down, I go down with the ship. I believe in this and I go down with it." I walked out and it was confirmed to me I was not to give up. I did not have that choice to give up. I went out, had t-shirts made, then came back, and gave them to the staff.

They said, "Failure is not an option." I said, "You wear that until you believe it. Failure is not an option here." I look back, and now we have more than a million dollars a year come in, just come in. People die and give us their entire wills and we have more money than it takes to run our organization, which is an amazing thing. Now it's fun, but it's not as great as it was during those hard times. That is when the real tests were passed.

Janet: Richard, if some of our listeners and readers want to participate in Christmas Box House projects and become some of your advocates, how do they go about doing that?

Richard: Contact me at my personal email which is: author@richardpaulevans.com.

Janet: What's the single most important idea you'd like to leave our readers with that you haven't discussed with all of us yet?

Richard: I think we discussed all of the things that were important. It comes back to me over and over, the idea of adversity. It is the difficult experiences, and your readers have difficult experiences in their lives, that give us a chance to shape and to grow.

Whatever you want to accomplish, to have a sense of destiny is the starting point. I had a complete sense of destiny with *The Christmas Box*. If you have that sense of destiny, it will lead you where you need to go.

That is the underlying tone of everything we talked about. Without it, if you don't believe there's a destiny or divinity to our lives, then it's all a crap shoot anyway.

Janet: I am with you 100%, and I love that you left all of us with that thought. To the extent you're in alignment with what I call God's will for you, you can't possibly have a desire, a passion that's not totally in alignment with what God's will is for you.

Richard: Absolutely.

To learn more about Richard Paul Evans and his Christmas Box Houses, go to:

www.richardpaulevans.com
www.thechristmasboxhouse.org

What were the key lessons from this interview about living your passion?

1. Unexpected support begins to show up when you're so aligned with what you're supposed to be doing, doors open in ways you couldn't have predicted.

2. Sometimes there's an advantage of doing it yourself, when you're passionate about it. For example, Richard's self-published book was more successful than if it had gone through a major publisher.

3. When you're passionate, you may not be good at what you're doing in the beginning. But if you have to do it to follow your passions, then experience will make you good at it.

4. Passion can be contagious. When people hear your passion, they want to be part of it.

5. Anytime you're following your passions, you're going to be tested. Things will show up to test how much you care about something.

6. When you're passionate, you will be willing to fight for your passions, to do uncomfortable things, to take chances, to risk everything.

7. We do not succeed in spite of our obstacles and challenges. We succeed precisely because of them.

8. Success comes from making mistakes and learning from them.

9. Fear is the opposite of faith. You can't have fear and faith at the same time. When you're ready to move, you let go of the fear.

10. When you're passionate, failure is not an option.

11. When you have a sense of destiny, it will lead you where you need to go.

How will you use these points in your own life starting now?

You can be part of the live teleaudience, absolutely FREE, when Healthy Wealthy nWise conducts interviews with amazing people like the one you just read. Go to:

http://www.healthywealthynwise.com/interview

There you can quickly and easily sign up to receive reminders on all of the incredible upcoming calls.

♥

9

JAY ABRAHAM

IT'S ABOUT EVERYONE ELSE

By: Janet Attwood

*Talking about **Jay Abraham**, Michael Basch, one of the founding officers of Federal Express, says:*

> "I've met only two marketing geniuses in my life. The first was Vince Fagan, the man who came up with 'When it absolutely, positively has to be there overnight—Fed Ex.' The second is Jay Abraham. Jay teaches you more workable, tangible, profitable techniques and strategies than you can probably apply in three lifetimes. But what he teaches you about mindset is his true gift of wealth."

Jay's clients credit him with adding billions of dollars in revenues to their income statements. To accomplish this feat, he's worked with over 10,000 small and medium-sized businesses.

It's no surprise that Forbes magazine listed him as one of the five top executive coaches in the world, saying Jay's specialty is, "Turning corporate underperformers into marketing and sales whizzes."

Jay has been acknowledged as a unique and distinctive authority in the field of business performance enhancement – and the maximizing and multiplying of business assets. He's been featured twice in Investors Business Daily, *which described Jay as someone who, "Knows how to maximize results with minimum effort."*

In addition, Jay has been written up in USA Today, the New York Times, the Los Angeles Times, the Washington Post, the San Francisco Chronicle, the OTC Stock Journal, National Underwriter, Entrepreneur, Success, Inc. *magazine, and many others.*

He's spawned an entire generation of marketing consultants and experts who credit him as their primary mentor as a result of his past Protégé and Consultant Training programs. Nearly 2,000 Web sites reference his successful work on the Internet alone.

Janet: Just a few weeks ago, you went through The Passion Test, so would you begin by sharing with our readers what you identified as your top passion?

Jay: I'd be happy to, Janet. First of all, I think the Test is very provocative and very revealing, and it's unlike anything else anyone has ever exposed me to.

You challenged me in a very revealing way.

The number one passion in my life is daily having an extraordinarily fluid relationship with my wife and children in all aspects of our lives together. That is the number one, triple most important area in my life.

Janet: That is so great. Have you found your passions are changing, as you grow older?

Jay: Yes, they are. I'm sure your readers represent a broad spectrum of ages, socio-economic representations, and goals—but for those of you who haven't achieved all your goals yet, irrespective of your age, one of the most wonderful realities is that material goals, when and if you achieve them, are not, by themselves, going to transform your life.

It's certainly nice to have enough economic security to be able to live where you want and eat what you want, and have some of the trappings you want, but once you get the "stuff" you want, you realize there's a lot more to life than just things, status and stature.

I've been fortunate, or unfortunate, however you look at it.

I've done a lot, Janet, I've had a lot, I've experienced a lot, and I really subordinated factors in my life that, as I've gotten older, as my health has become more of a concern to me, as I've watched children grow and loved ones die, and seen the ones most important to me not be as close as I would have liked—I've slowed down and re-calibrated what's relevant. It's relevant to me at a different level than it might be to somebody else.

Janet: So you've achieved the financial success and fame you'd wanted in the past, yes?

Jay: I have achieved a nice degree of it. We always aspire for more, but yes, I'm very happy, I've made a lot of money and I've become known around the world by millions and millions of people, and I don't know if most people could ask for more than that.

Janet: What are the other passions you wrote down? The first one was having an extraordinary, fluid relationship with your wife and children. What's number two?

Jay: Having balance in my life. Same thing, I used to be a workaholic and monstrously committed. I had a tremendous capacity to accomplish work, I'd work eighteen hours a day, seven days a week, and have meetings at two in the morning.

Now, though, if my wife calls and says, "Let's go to lunch," unless I have a very, very important meeting, I'll stop and do that, because in the scope of forever, that's more important. I want balance—economic, intellectual, spiritual, physical, sexual—all kinds of balanced stimulation at a level that's very healthy.

Janet: Let me ask you, because this whole conversation is about passion, is being passionate about what you're doing important to you?

Jay: It's everything to me. I think if you can't be passionate about something or someone, you shouldn't even have that in your life because you're stealing the experience from them and from you. Why do anything half invested? Why do anything and accept half of the outcome, half the result, half of the payoff?

There is a great payoff from being passionate. Passionate is probably the most selfish thing you can be because you get so much more out of it.

Janet: What role has passion played in your success in life?

Jay: I will tell you the role it's played, in the positive and in the negative. In the positive, my passion for wanting to see a business owner be so much more than they are, my passion for knowing how much more was possible from the day, from the investment, from the opportunity, from an advertisement, from a competitive environment.

My passion for having a vision for somebody that was greater than they even had for themselves because I knew what they could do, my passion for having enough faith in a client or a business that I knew how much more they could contribute to their community, and their marketplace, and their prospective client, was what drove billions and billions of dollars to be created, because I believed in them and ultimately they believed more deeply in themselves.

In my personal life I haven't been as passionate. I put too much of my time in my business and I've lost relationships. I can say it goes both ways. Lack of passion costs you dearly and sometimes you don't know the cost because it's a compound bill that when it comes due is very painful. I think passion needs to be balanced and passion needs to be universal.

If you can't be passionate, if you can't really fall in love with what you're doing, who you're doing it for or with, and the result of it, shame on you. Do it full out. That's my opinion.

Janet: What can our readers learn from your experience?

Jay: If I were you, each and every one of you reading this, I would try this Passion Test. Tomorrow morning, start looking at the people you interact with in your life. If you have a wife or a husband, or a significant other, if you have children, family members, that you normally are frustrated with, tired of, not appreciative of, don't get what you think you want from, feel choked or, claustrophobic about—start looking at what's great about them.

Find something that's really neat about them. Find the one thing about them that's really cool, really interesting, really impressive, really amazing, really wonderful, really remarkable and keep doing that every day. Think about the thing about them that you love among everything else. Think about what is the most impressive thing. Think about their greatest attribute, whether you admire it or not, whether it's their work ethic or their discipline or their joy of living, or whatever it is, and start appreciating and understanding them.

It's your job in life to observe, examine, appreciate, understand and respect how many different ways everyone else sees the same thing you're going through.

Maybe you don't agree one hundred percent, but if you appreciate it, if you respect it, if you examine it, if you observe it objectively and without pre-judgment, it just makes life so much more dimensional, fascinating, fun, educational, and informative.

Janet: How can our listeners enjoy great success at the same time as that?

Jay: The key of all life is value. Value is not what you get, it's what you give. It's figuring out what's important to other people, not just to you. Now how do I think I'm going to have an extraordinary, fluid relationship with my wife and children? Do you think it will work if I yell, "Hey you guys, I want to be connected"?

Do you think that's going to do it? Or am I going to have a higher probability of success by first figuring out what's important to them, what they like, what they enjoy, what rings their bell, what rocks their boat, what brings them happiness —and trying to connect with them on that level, first and foremost?

I always made a fortune when I put the businesses I was serving, and my client's needs, ahead of mine. I always had a great relationship, a great romance, great sex, whatever you want, when I put my spouse's needs, interests and, goals ahead of mine. I mean, it's real simple.

It's very elegant in its purity. Think about what's important to them, whoever "they" are, whether it's business, whether it's your employer. Most people don't understand that.

If you work for somebody else, figure out what problems they're struggling with, figure out what's going to make them more secure, what's going to make them more successful. With somebody above you, figure out what's going to get them a raise, what's going to get them a promotion, what's going to get them acknowledgement, and that will get you what you want.

It's pretty simple really, but we're so consumed about us, us, us. The real fast track path to getting everything, anything and more than everything you want is putting others ahead of what you want and focusing on their needs, their wants, their desires, and fulfilling them.

Janet: Is it fair to say that one of your passions has been to figure out what others want?

Jay: Yes. It's not manipulative, it's great joy. I am lucky. I don't have everything I want, but I have more than most people have. I have exotic cars, I've got a huge home, I've got a beach house, I've traveled around the world twenty times. I've got people always offering me free first class tickets. I have a lot of stuff, don't you think?

Janet: Yes, absolutely, more than almost anyone I know.

Jay: You know I'm more interested in figuring out what turns other people on than me. It's greatly fulfilling and it's much more fun to help them grow, develop, gain fulfillment and enrichment. I get more out of it, frankly.

I don't believe there is such a thing as altruism. I think we get back massively from everything we do.

Janet: Can you remember a time when you weren't living your passion and how that impacted your life? What showed up for you? How was your success?

Jay: My business almost collapsed, my marriage almost collapsed and my health almost collapsed. Oh, and I lost most of my money. Other than that it was OK (laughs).

Janet: Then how did you get back on track?

Jay: Well, I hit rock bottom emotionally. I went and looked around my life, figuratively speaking, and thought, "Wow I have a chance to influence a ton of people in my business. Wow, I have this lovely, beautiful, loving, dimensional wife. Wow, I've got these gorgeous kids. Wow, I have these really wonderful and dimensional friends.

Wow, I live in this wonderful part of the world where I can be free. Wow, when I think, my brain functions. When I've got an itch, my fingers all work and I can scratch my nose. I'm a pretty lucky fellow.

Janet: Why do you think most people give up on their dreams? What is your advice to those who have?

Jay: Three things.

People give up on their dreams because they don't have a clear path to follow.

Everyone reading this probably has some level of interest or hobby. It may be tennis, it may be gardening, it may be sailing, it may be you name it. The odds are exceedingly high, and in fact, almost certainly probable, that the first time you each tried it you weren't masterful at it. You had to keep refining it and improving it, in fact it might have even been laughable. It might have been a joke.

I can remember, whether it be my business acumen, my athletic capability, just about everything I was a joke at, and if I'd stopped there and not gotten back on the horse and recommitted to it, I probably would have never enjoyed all the joy and the wonderment. Most people set high lofty aspirations for themselves. They don't understand that little steps of progress are profound.

Let me give you a firsthand experience, which may help.

I used to be very frustrated when I did seminars. I would bring someone to a seminar who was at, let's say, base level zero. I would stretch them to as high as my arm could reach in the course of three or five days.

Then they'd go back and they'd drop down to maybe just ten percent of where they were and I'd be heartbroken. One time I was talking to a colleague of mine who was a psychologist and he said, "Jay, you're focusing on the wrong stat. You're looking at how high you got them and how far they fell, instead of looking at where they started and how high they got after that."

I think we all set for ourselves such a lofty and probably unrealistic time line and achievement objective, that when we don't achieve it instantly, we get heartbroken, we get frustrated, we get embittered, we feel impotent mentally or capability wise.

I think when we don't get the response, the result, the feedback, we're looking for, we recoil back to the sanctity and certainty of our mundane, mediocre, unfulfilled life, and we resign ourselves to that being our fatalistic destiny instead of saying, "I executed wrong, let's try again, I've got to adjust and recalibrate."

Even an airplane flying across country, if you left it to its own devices, would go off track. There's no one and nothing I've ever seen be great or be monstrously successful the first time at bat.

But most people want to be Casey at the bat. When they strike out they basically want to take their ball and go home, and it's tragic really because so many people could enjoy such a richer, happier, and more successful life—a greater body, a greater marriage, a greater sexual life, and greater self esteem. Instead they drop out the first time it doesn't feel good or the first time it doesn't look good or the first time they don't get the feedback they want or the first time they feel awkward. That's what I think, does that make sense?

Janet: Absolutely.

Jay, I keep thinking of this question: If you imagine that our readers are your biggest client and they've hired you to make their life the most successful it can be, what questions would you ask them to ask themselves to realize their dream?

Jay: The first is I want to know why they have the dream. Sometimes I'll see somebody who's got the desire to have the fastest growing business in the world. I'll say, "Why do you have that desire?" They'll say, "I don't know." Then I'll ask, "Is it because you need acknowledgement, because you have a weak ego, because you have low self esteem, or because you want that business to create great wealth or great income?"

They probably hadn't thought about it. If they did answer the former, I'll say, "Well, what would get you that acknowledgement easier, faster, with less effort? Let's examine the options and the opportunities and the alternatives." Most people don't have a clue about how many easier, faster, safer, more enjoyable ways there are to get to their goal, because they don't know what their goal really is and they don't know why they have it.

A lot of people want to have a big company only because they want to make a million dollars. If I can show you easier, faster, safer, less stressful ways to make the million dollars with ten people instead of a hundred and ten maybe it's not what you want, but you should get clear on why you want something.

What is it you want, why do you want it, what alternatives can give you the same thing or better, easier, faster, safer and more enjoyably? That's the first thing I would ask. That goes to career also.

Next is what are you willing to give to the marketplace in order to get it, because there is compensation for everything. You don't get unless you give. Most people don't realize it—you want to be massively successful, what are you going to give to the world, what are you going to give to your employer, what are you going to give to your wife, to your husband, to your children, in order to get it? That's a really profound and very provocative question. Does that make sense?

Janet: It does.

You have a reputation Jay, of helping people create phenomenal results, we all know that. Yet, the advice you're giving doesn't sound like hard, practical results or even steps, so how do you get from all of this attitude stuff to results?

Jay: Well, when you get into the business-building dynamic, it's surprisingly simple. There are a couple of realizations that if you'll make them, everything else will fall in line. Here's something that's tangible and specific. There are three ways, and only three ways, to grow any business and really any career.

In the business, you add more buyers – more clients, you get them to spend more money or buy more things, and you get them to come back more often or get more utilization or utility or repurchase value out of them.

In your job, you get more admirers or more devotees or more fans or more influence or more points of influence. You get people to turn to you to do more things that they're dependent on. That will always produce greater income.

In making money, most people have only one approach that they depend on, and it's very limited and very linear. I try to build multiple pillars of income for people—multiple streams of income. In the business arena for example, most people have one revenue or income-generating or buyer-generating process. I have most people get eight or nine and they radically multiply their success.

There is a concept called the "strategy of preeminence" that I teach. It takes about two hours but I will give you the ninety-second version.

First, you establish yourself and your relationship with everybody as their most trusted advisor. As their advisor, your job is to give them the best reason, most heartfelt external perspective on what's best for them. You have a "you attitude," "you" meaning "them" and not yourself. Always focus on them.

Number two, you try to put into words the gnawing feelings, the desires, the frustrations they feel that are never verbalized.

Number three, you tell them the truth as you see it.

Number four, you never let them do things that are not in their best interest.

Number five, you tell them what you see life to be in your own words, and you don't hold back even if they won't like you for it, because you see yourself as their most trusted advisor.

Number six, I told you, you fall in love with them, not your business or your product.

Number seven, realize that it's not what you say that makes people buy from you, that makes people hire you, that makes people give you raises, it's how much more value you can give them that they desire, prize, and really want.

Number eight, you make yourself stand out as the only viable solution they've got, to a problem you alone understand and verbalize, or an opportunity you alone see and can really put words to.

In addition, you stop working harder for your business or your job than you let the business and the job work for you. You do that by understanding how to harness the power of geometry. Geometry is harnessed when you let multiple activities work together to produce a geometric or exponential result.

You will find that in order to be successful you have to first want to make other people successful, in order to be loved, you have to first love, in order to be interesting you have to first be interested. The mere opposite of what you want is what you have to give first and then you will get back the desired result or outcome in droves. Does that help?

Janet: Yes, thank you Jay.

What other advice can you give our readers to help them find their passions and create balance in their lives today?

Jay: Stretch, ask a lot of questions, examine a lot of different realities. We used to do seminars where we'd have five, six or seven hundred people there, and they would pay me $5,000 to $25,000 apiece.

The first thing I would do on the second day is go around the room and ask them what they absolutely love. Usually people love something, they love to eat, they love to watch sports, they love to have sex, they love to do something, maybe they had a hobby.

Whatever they loved I'd make them do something polar

opposite. If somebody liked macramé I'd give them a book on wrestling or on tattooing or on fly fishing, or I'd give them a magazine about it and make them read two chapters or two articles and come back and report to the rest of the room something absolutely fascinating and remarkably interesting about that. This would help them see how much more there is to life, how many more facets and elements and possibilities.

I would say to everybody, experience a lot more of life, observe a lot more facets, examine how many different ways or facets of fun, of happiness, of purpose, of enrichment there are, other than the one's or the two's or the three's you have allowed yourself so far. Don't be judgmental, be observational, be clinical, just observe for a while, and it is impossible not to have it penetrate your soul and your heart. It can't not work.

Janet: You know we believe strongly in intention to manifest outcomes, so what is your current, most important project, Jay? And what intention would you like us here at *Healthy Wealthy nWise*, as well as our readers, to hold for you?

Jay: I have three intentions. First of all, I have not been as wonderful a husband and father as I could have been, and I would really like to be world class at that. My idea of world class is moot and irrelevant, it's what world class means to the ones I want to do it for, so I have to be able to be externally focused.

Number two is, I want to basically make everybody in the world see how much more is possible for them and from their efforts and their opportunities and their daily expenditures of energy and effort. The tragedy in life is how little they accept.

I think you had Bob Proctor on—I saw his picture on one of your magazine covers. I like when he said, "Most people in life struggle, totally and obsessively, with the wrong non-verbalized questions."

They're constantly challenging and questioning themselves

on the issue, "Am I really worthy of the goal I set? Can I really be more successful? Can I really be happy? Can I really be a good husband, a good father, a good friend, a good lover?

"Can I really have a business that's successful? Can I really expect to gain financial security? Can I really ever hope to live in a bigger house? Can I ever hope to get rid of this weight? Can I ever hope to be loved by somebody?"

He said those are absolutely the wrong questions to ask.

The right question is not, "Am I worthy of the goal," but, "Is the goal worthy of me?"

When you realize how much more you can do, how much more you can impact, how much more you can contribute, how much more you can achieve, how much more you can enrich people at all levels—tangibly, intangibly, spiritually, emotionally, physically—by your body of work, by being on this planet, by interacting, you are going to raise the bar, you're going to knock out all the false ceilings. My goal is to do that for a lot of people.

My third goal is absolutely to manifest in this intention, I want this expenditure, this contribution, this commitment, and this transference of an hour of my life to some number of thousands of people to have made a difference. I want it not to have them feel good or warm or fuzzy or smile, I want them to do something, I want them to transform themselves, I want them to forever be haunted by my message and have it compel them to take the continuous little, easy steps forward.

When they have a little setback or a big one, to dust themselves off, go back in the ring, keep pursuing their goal and not be self-consumed, but have it be externally focused because that's the greatest accelerator and enhancer of achievement, of fulfillment, of enrichment you'll ever get.

Janet: Jay, it's so easy to see why you are such a giant in your field by the degree of heart you put into this hour we've had together. Let me ask you one last question: What is the single most important idea you would like to leave our readers with that we haven't yet discussed this evening?

Jay: That the biggest reason most people don't achieve the enrichment on both financial and emotional levels is their self-focus. It isn't about you, it's about everyone else, and when you make everyone else's life better, your life automatically opens up and expands monstrously. It's about falling in love with other people, what you're doing for them, and getting clear on what your life is all about.

How in the name of whomever you hold dear can you expect to get anything more if you're not clear about what it is? It's like saying, "I'm sitting here, Janet, and I'm trying to go to some place in North America." It's like saying, "I don't know where I am now, I don't know where I'm going, I don't know how I'm going to get there."

As opposed to saying, "Janet, I'm in Los Angeles. I want to be in Chicago and I want to be there in five hours. I know there are a lot of options. I could drive, I could take the train, I could take a jet, I could take a private plane or I could take a helicopter." With all these options, nobody on this call has the right to be disappointed with anything in their life, if they haven't first and foremost gone through this process.

It's audacious and ludicrous to flagellate yourself for what you haven't achieved if you don't first go through this very clarifying, expedient and absolutely immutable and unerring process that will get you whatever it is you want faster, easier; and you won't just achieve it, you will easily and profoundly exceed whatever you set for yourself if you turn your attention to what you can give to others.

Janet: Jay, thank you so much.

Jay: You're welcome. You do know this is not what I usually do and this is not the topic I usually talk about.

Janet: I know, and it was so much fun to talk to you about this. Thank you so much for playing with us.

To learn more about the work of Jay Abraham, visit:

www.abraham.com

What were the key lessons from this interview about living your passion?

1. Material goals, by themselves, are not going to transform your life.

2. Why do anything half invested? There is a great payoff from being passionate.

3. Lack of passion costs you dearly and sometimes you don't know the cost because it's a compound bill that can be very painful when it comes due.

4. Find the one thing in those you interact with in your life which is really cool, really interesting, really impressive, really remarkable and use these things to start appreciating and understanding those closest to you.

5. The key of all life is value. Value is not what you get, it's what you give. It's figuring out what's important to other people, not just you.

6. The real fast track to getting everything, anything, and more than everything you want is putting others ahead of what you want and focusing on their needs, their wants, their desires, and fulfilling them.

7. It's much more fun to help others grow, develop, gain fulfillment and enrichment.

8. People give up on their dreams because of three things:
   #1 – they don't have a clear path to follow
   #2 – they set such lofty time lines and objectives, they're not achievable
   #3 – they give up the first time things don't go the way they'd hoped

9. When you want to realize your dream, the first question to ask is, "Why do you have that dream?"

10. Second, what alternatives can give you the same thing or better—easier, faster, more safely and more enjoyably?

11. Third, what are you willing to give to the marketplace in order to get it?

12. There are three ways and only three ways to grow any business, or any career. In business, you add more buyers/more clients, get them to spend more money, and get them to come back more often. In a career, you get more admirers or points of influence, you get people to turn to you to do more things that they're dependent on.

13. The strategy of preeminence: One, you establish yourself and your relationship with others as their most trusted advisor. Two, put into words the gnawing feelings, desires, frustrations they feel that are never verbalized. Three, you tell them the truth as you see it. Four, you never let them do things that are not in their best interest. Five, you tell them what you see life to be in your own words, without holding back. Six, you fall in love with them, not your business or your product. Seven, you realize that what makes people buy from you, hire you, give you raises, is

how much value you can give them that they desire, prize and really want. Eight, you demonstrate that you offer the only viable solution to a problem they've got.

14. In order to be successful, you have to first want to make others successful. To be loved, you have to first love. To be interesting, you have to first be interested.

15. To find your passions and create balance, stretch, ask a lot of questions and examine a lot of different realities.

16. Don't be judgmental, be observational, be clinical. Just observe for a while, and it's impossible not to have it penetrate your soul and your heart.

17. The right question is not, "Am I worthy of the goal," but, "Is the goal worthy of me?"

18. The biggest reason most people don't achieve enrichment on both financial and emotional levels is their self-focus. It isn't about you, it's about everyone else, and when you make everyone else's life better, your life automatically opens up.

How will you use these points in your own life starting now?

You can be part of the live teleaudience, absolutely FREE, when Healthy Wealthy nWise conducts interviews with amazing people like the one you just read. Go to:

http://www.healthywealthynwise.com/interview

There you can quickly and easily sign up to receive reminders on all of the incredible upcoming calls.

10

DR. DENIS WAITLEY

PLAY TO WIN FROM WITHIN

By: Chris Attwood and Tellman Knudson

Denis Waitley *is one of the most respected authors, speakers and productivity consultants on high performance and human achievement in the world. Over ten million copies of his audio programs have been sold in over fourteen different languages. He's the author of fourteen books and several international best sellers, including* Seeds of Greatness, Being the Best, The Winner's Edge, The Joy of Working, *and* Empires of the Mind.

His audio album, The Psychology of Winning, *is the all-time, best-selling program on self mastery. Dr. Waitley has counseled winners in every single field, from Apollo astronauts to Super Bowl champions, from Olympic athletes to sales achievers to government leaders. He's served as chairman of psychology on the US Olympic Committee's Sports Medicine Council.*

Dr. Waitley is a graduate of the U.S. Naval Academy in Annapolis, Maryland and holds a Ph.D. in Human Behavioral Psychology.

Tellman Knudson, founder of ListCrusade.com, conducted this interview with Chris Attwood. List Crusade has become its own success story as Tellman has assembled some of the top authors, speakers, trainers, and Internet marketers in one place to share their knowledge.

Tellman: As you know, this series is called The Passions of Real Life Legends. Will you take a few moments to tell us how you went about discovering your own passions and specifically, how they led you to the work you do today?

Dr. Waitley: That's a great question to begin with. First, I'll have to say people need to understand it's never too late to discover your passion, and most multimillionaires are made after the age of 50. If you're somewhere between 20 and 40 and haven't become a multimillionaire or achieved all you want to achieve, don't worry. Some of the greatest people in history did it much later in life because many times, what I'm going to say right now didn't occur to them, or maybe they buried it deep down.

When I was about ten months old, my mom said she put me out in my little jump swing in the front lawn and people came by. She said I'd bounce up and down laughing, and babble some nonsense to everyone in earshot, and I guess nothing's changed because it seems as if I still do that today!

By the time I was about 3 to 5, I was telling stories and singing songs for neighbors, for cookies. By the time I was 14, I was mayor of my junior high and giving speeches. By the time I was 16, I was student body president. At that time, there was no such thing as a career in public speaking, and the Korean War was on, so I gave up all of my early passions and stirrings.

I went to the Naval Academy in Annapolis and became a warrior and a defender. I found myself, in the 1960s, as a carrier-based, top gun pilot, and my training was to deliver nuclear weapons. Yet my true passion was to develop people rather than defend against them or destroy them.

Another thing happened to me. I was raised in a poor family with a lot of alcoholism and divorce, but I rode my bike about twenty miles one way every Saturday because my grandmother was an optimist and she kindled my passion by telling me I was going to go forward, do good, be something.

She would tell me, as we were planting the victory garden, that we were planting the seeds of greatness. She said the seeds of greatness are ideas you learn from people who've been great in their service to others. My grandmother was my inspiration to dig up my passion, which had been subdued for many years as a carrier-based pilot.

I always thought back to my grandma, planting seeds of greatness. That's why I think passion is what drives all of us. You have to stay true to your passion, even though you may get off on a tangent when you're chasing some money for your early responsibilities after college or when you get married. That passion still underlies everything else and therein lies the secret to your destiny.

Tellman: I know you personally have worked with heads of corporations, Olympic athletes, POWs, network marketers and people with all sorts of different backgrounds. In your experience, what role does passion play in an individual's success? Can you give us some examples of how that works out for people?

Dr. Waitley: I think I can, Tellman. Ross Perot was my big brother at the Naval Academy and he went on to become a billionaire with Electronic Data Systems. He was always a man of passion. Ray Kroc was my next door neighbor, and as you remember, he founded McDonald's when he was 54, so it's never too late. Ray Kroc always said, "Love it or leave it."

I think back to the role passion plays. Let's look back at

Steven Spielberg doing his little home movies. Andrew Lloyd Weber, as we remember, he wrote *Cats*, *Evita*, and did the *Phantom of the Opera*. When he was 9 years old, he had a little home theater with puppets.

Steve Cauthen, who won the Triple Crown at the age of 17, was riding a bale of hay around his farm and his father said, "Put that bale in the truck." Steve Cauthen said, "I will as soon as I win the Kentucky Derby."

My good friend, Jacques Cousteau, before he died, told me he had broken both arms and was watching a water spider. A little water spider was taking a bubble of air down to her babies in a lake, and he had to swim. Jacques wanted to be an astronaut, but he broke his arms and had to become an aquanaut instead. He saw the bubble of air in this little spider, wished he could breathe underwater, and invented the aqua lung.

As I've looked at people like Bill Gates of Microsoft, Fred Smith of Federal Express and every great inventor or innovator, they weren't trying to make money. They had an inner fire of passion to drive them, rather than a desire for wealth. That's why I believe most successful people achieve their greatness because they have something to express inside.

It's not the idea of a pet rock to make a lot of money, but many of them earn a tremendous amount of money and respect. I think that Thomas Edison, Estée Lauder, Walt Disney, Oprah, and Sam Walton—they made a lot of money, but far more than thinking about money when they were doing it, the key to their success was their passion.

It was this inner drive of creating or providing something excellent in a product or service. They were all motivated by the desire to produce the very best that was inside of them. I call that the "*Stradivarius effect*." Antonio Stradivari made violins for other people to play.

He couldn't play the violin very well, but when he made a

violin, he signed his name to it and said, "If you like me, refer me, and if you like me, renew me. If you don't like it, I'll fix it for you, but play me and play the music of your life on my instrument." He didn't realize that by signing his name to his work and living his own passion, his name and work would outlive him and each violin would be worth more than a million bucks, 350 years later.

To me, the Stradivarius ethic is the way I love to live, by really uncovering and discovering your passion. That is the secret to people who make millions. Even Donald Trump—don't think it's just the money—it's the art of the deal with the Donald. Sure, the Donald has an ego and he likes to do his *"you're fired"* and all of that, but the Donald is a deal maker and he loves the deal. I think passion drives us all much more than we think.

Tellman: When you're talking about passion and highly successful people, I think great examples of that are Olympic athletes. People go for years, from being on a high school team to being on a college team, continuing to push through, going to a semi-pro and then a pro level.

They build themselves up in their abilities until they reach the status where they can compete in the Olympics. That's pure passion. There's no way you can deny that. For people like Olympic athletes, one really has to believe in their natural, God-given talent. It has so much to do with determining what their passions are. If that is true, do everyone's talents lead them to their passions?

Dr. Waitley: Boy, is that a good question. That's a loaded question that is a double-edged sword. First of all, talent and passion are definitely the twin powers. They're the twin towers of power. Sometimes we discover our talents at a very early age, which is true for most of the Olympians. Most of the Olympians had a coach.

First, they loved what they were doing, they probably were

really great; then a coach said, *"I see world class potential in you,"* and the coach gave them the correct swing or the correct way to do it, and they found they could hone that natural talent, with passion, not their parents' passion, because too often parents tend to push their children in a direction so the parents can vicariously live their lives over again.

It isn't always the talent that creates the passion. Sometimes the passion uncovers the talent. I've been working with Olympians for many years, helping mentally train them. At the world class level, it's almost all mental. You have these natural talents, but at that moment of truth, the mind over muscle wins.

I think back to my good friend Bill Toomey. A lot of people don't remember Bill Toomey, but he was a school teacher. He was at the Olympics in Munich, Germany, sitting in the stands, watching this German win the decathlon. Twelve hundred days later, four years later, he won the decathlon in Mexico City, and I was there. That's because he was training in the rain.

The high jump took place in the rain and because the German fouled out in the rain, he won. Here's the guy who was a school teacher with a passion for sports. He was a coach and a school teacher, but he never really uncovered those tremendous talents until he did a four-year deal on becoming an Olympian.

A person like Scott Hamilton, for example, overcame a life-threatening disease to become a champion figure skater. So sometimes, the passion for problem-solving or something that we're making up for gives us the motivation to dig out our talents. Sometimes our passion comes first because we express an interest in something that excites us, and that passion uncovers the natural, undeveloped abilities.

For the most part, I think if you dust off your childhood passions and think back to the talents you had, let's say when you were 7 to 15. Think about the things you loved to do as a child and then think about your current hobbies. As you think about the things you love to do in your off hours, or the things you loved to do as a child, therein will lie your natural talents.

Natural talents begin to blossom early, but they get nipped in the bud by what I call "the parent, the peer group and the professor" who tell us we should be concentrating on something like computers that will earn us money, instead of chasing this crazy passion of ours, and the talent in that passion which may be the key to riches untold.

I think hobbies are normally the best examples of talents, and childhood talents and hobbies will give us a combination of blending passion and talent together.

Tellman: You've worked very closely at times with the Dell Computer Corporation. I'm wondering if you'd be willing to take a few minutes and share the Michael Dell story. It's a very interesting one. More importantly, how can people apply the same principles, ideas and concepts from that story in their own lives?

Dr. Waitley: I could give the whole call on Michael Dell. He bugs me; he drives me absolutely crazy because here's a guy, who was born in 1965. In 1965, I was a brilliant psychologist. Where have I been? I don't have a clue. He was sucking a pacifier, crawling around in his diapers, when I was already thinking of myself as successful.

Somehow, in the next thirty years, he became the richest person in the world under the age of 40.

The first thing he did was get a stamp collection and form the Michael Dell stamp auction. The next thing he did was quickly try to take the GED exam so he didn't have to go to school. He had somebody come over to give him the equivalency exam, and his mother said, "He's taking his bath."

The woman said, "I thought he was a Vietnam veteran." She said, "No, he's in the third grade." She said, "Oh my gosh! Well, I came here to give him the…" and he came out in his bath robe and said, "Why can't I take it? Why do I have to go to school? It's a waste of time."

We should have known then that Michael Dell was going to be a special guy because the next thing he did was sell newspaper subscriptions. You know what the business is, everyone will tell you, it's the number of calls you make that will make you successful. He didn't want to buy just that.

He wanted to be high-probability, prospect oriented. We all need to find out who wants to buy what we're selling. What did Michael Dell do? He didn't knock on every door in Houston. Instead, he went to the post office and the bank and he went to the library, and he found out who had just bought a home, who had just gotten married, who had just moved into the neighborhood, and then he formed the Michael Dell Welcome Wagon and gave them the *Houston Post*.

The first day they moved in, he said, "Do you want it all during the week or on Sunday?" He gave them the alternate close, showed up at their door the minute they were moving in. He said, "I'm not going to knock on people's doors who probably already have the newspaper. I'm going to find people who are just moving in to upscale neighborhoods, who want the newspaper."

He drove to the University of Texas in a new, white BMW with an Apple IIe computer on his lap. He took it apart and found out there's nothing different in computers, so he just made them to order. He saw a Burger King ad and it said, "Have it your way."

"Sesame seed bun, hold the mayo, hold the lettuce…" So he made computers to order and he had a little business going. He quit school in his freshman year and the rest is history. The interesting thing about him is that he was first into retail for computers and first out.

In 1990, Dell Computer was sold in all the ComputerLand stores and in 1991 they were no longer sold there. Why? Because he knew that direct, direct, direct was the battle cry of the future, eliminating the middle person, eliminating the inefficiency, giving it to them their way, quick.

Real time inventory, off the shelf, but make them think they're getting it exactly like they're designing it—design it for the customer. He's been able to move from mass marketing to *"me"* marketing by giving each individual what they want and doing a desire analysis in advance.

He's the master of customization, of *"me"* marketing and of saving time. He now owns the lion's share of the PC market and the lion's share of this whole industry and it's all because he's impatient, he wants to save people time and money, and he wants to give it to them their way.

I'll tell you, he's really a study for me to figure out how I can eliminate all the extra steps in my own life. What I'm doing is taking an audit and saying, "What routines am I going through that are a total waste of time and are not leading me toward the achievement of my goals?" I'm starting to get rid of the dead wood in the time I'm spending majoring in minors and reading emails that don't mean anything.

Tellman: I know those different habits we all get into, whether they're physical habits or thought-pattern habits, can definitely rule our lives. Especially when people have intensely negative or traumatizing-type situations, those things can throw you for a loop. One of the things you've specialized in is working with returning POWs. What was that like? What types of lessons can we learn from those experiences?

Dr. Waitley: I did my dissertation on why no American prisoner ever escaped from a minimum-security camp, but many prisoners escaped from a maximum-security camp. The reason is that leaders are always put in a maximum-security camp because they're always trying to get home or get out or get a plan. People who are not motivated are put in minimum-security camps because they know they can't get out and they don't try.

What I learned from POWs is that we all, no matter where we are, are living in our imaginations and we're caught in this world between our ears. We're all doing within while we're doing without. The problem with a POW is that he's not an Olympian, because an Olympian is training for the games he knows he wants to participate in.

An astronaut is training for the moon shot, but a prisoner of war has to train while he's in prison, not knowing whether he's going to get out or not, but believing that he is. What the POWs did is rehearsed positive things by recall and precall. I call it "instant replay of past success." When things are not going well, you need to replay your success.

Then you need to project in your imagination where you want to be, because the mind can't distinguish between simulated activity and real activity. So that's why I've always told the story of Colonel George Hall, who was a four-handicap golfer. He always played one round of golf in his imagination, in his eight-by-eight cell, with black pajamas, bare feet and a pail and a plate of rice.

He never went outside, his teeth rotted, his eyes went bad, and he got atrophied and withered, but he played one round of golf, very well incidentally, in his imagination. He played every putt, every stroke; he played games that the pros had played and he played games that he had played.

He played in his mind, and for some reason, when you play it in your mind, you create a pattern in your brain. When he came back, he played in the New Orleans Open and shot a 76, four over par, right onto his handicap. The news media was astounded and said, "Congratulations—beginner's re-entry luck!" He said, "Luck, are you kidding? I never three-putted the green in five and a half years of solitary confinement."

What I learn from POWs is if you get in the habit of feeling you're never going to get out, you may never get out. It's an imaginary prison as well as a real prison that we live in. Therefore, you really have to do within when you're doing without and create the habit pattern and experience of a winner, so that when you actually get there, it's like old home week, and it's like nothing new.

Therefore, it's so comfortable to succeed; it's because you've been through so many dress rehearsals. The POWs taught me that dress rehearsal can take place. Even in the most trying and negative circumstances, you can still play to win from within.

Tellman: Wow. That's a pretty powerful concept when you're using your mind in a way that can literally change the results you're getting in your life and whatever you're doing. With that in mind, what's the single biggest, most important idea you'd like to leave people with?

Dr. Waitley: I guess the idea I'd like to leave everyone with is that you have to believe you're as good as the best, but not necessarily better than the rest. That's what I say, "Denis, you're as good as the best, but no better than the rest." In other words, winners believe in their passion when that's all they have to hang on to.

You have to believe in that passion when you really don't have a track record that shows you shouldn't believe in it—you still need to believe in it because the passion is what's going to drive you to success. Failure is always a detour rather than a dead end. It's an event, not a person.

I've always looked at failure as a learning experience or target correction. I've got so much failure in my life that if failure were fertilizer, I'd have big bags of horse manure all over my room. However, failure is the fertilizer of success because it enables you to mulch it, lay it down and grow future ideas without making the same mistakes. Look at a mistake as something you're not going to repeat.

Finally, your self worth will, to a large extent, determine your eventual net worth. In other words, you will earn and accumulate what you believe you're worthy of having. Unless you're worth it, you won't be worth the effort that it takes to get it or do it.

To learn more about the work of Dr. Denis Waitley, visit:

www.waitley.com

What were the key lessons from this interview about living your passion?

1. It's never too late to discover your passion. Most multimillionaires are made after the age of 50.

2. Successful people achieve their greatness because they have something to express inside. They are motivated by the desire to produce the very best that is inside of them.

3. Talent and passion are the twin towers of power.

4. It isn't always talent that creates passion. Sometimes passion uncovers talent.

5. Sometimes the passion to overcome something we're making up for uncovers our talents.

6. The things you loved to do as a child provide clues to your natural talents.

7. Find ways to save people time and money, and give it to them their way, the way they want it—Michael Dell's secrets to success..

8. Time management: What routines am I going through that are a total waste of time and are not leading me toward the achievement of my goals?

9. We all live in our imaginations and are caught in the world between our ears. We create our world outside from what we are doing inside.

10. When things are not going well, you need to replay your success, then project in your imagination where you want to be, because the mind can't distinguish between simulated activity and real activity.

11. Create the habit pattern and experience of a winner inside, so when you get there on the outside, it's like old home week. It feels so comfortable to succeed because you've been through so many dress rehearsals.

12. Believe you're as good as the best, but not better than the rest.

13. Failure is a detour, not a dead end. It is the fertilizer of future success.

14. Your self worth will determine your eventual net worth. You will earn and accumulate what you believe you're worthy of having.

How will you use these points in your own life starting now?

You can be part of the live teleaudience, absolutely FREE, when Healthy Wealthy nWise conducts interviews with amazing people like the one you just read. Go to:

http://www.healthywealthynwise.com/interview

There you can quickly and easily sign up to receive reminders on all of the incredible upcoming calls.

11

STEPHEN M. R. COVEY

MOVING AT THE SPEED OF TRUST

By: Chris Attwood

Stephen M. R. Covey *was personally responsible for the strategy that propelled his father's book, Dr. Stephen R. Covey's: The 7 Habits of Highly Effective People, to become the number one, influential business book of the 20th century, according to CEO magazine. As CEO of Covey Leadership Center, he grew that company into the largest leadership development firm in the world.*

During his tenure, Covey Leadership Center went from $55 million in revenues to $112 million annually. Profits increased twelve times during the same period. When he took over, the company was valued at $2.4 million. Within three years he had grown shareholder value to $160 million and orchestrated a merger with Franklin Quest to create Franklin Covey.

He has now co-founded his own consultancy firm, CoveyLink, and is recognized as a leading authority in creating high trust, high performance organizations.

His new book, The Speed of Trust, *to be released in Fall, 2006, represents a major contribution to the understanding of one of the key components of high performance individuals and organizations.*

Chris: Let's begin with our theme for "The Passions of Real Life Legends." How did you discover your passions, the things that are most important to you in your life? How did that happen?

Stephen: I really discovered these twice, and the second time, knew it even better than the first time. The first time, I had spent a few years doing a variety of different professional work assignments. I'd been a real estate developer with a great real estate development company. I'd done a little bit of investment banking.

I enjoyed these activities. I enjoyed the excitement and the deal making, but I still sensed there was much more I could be doing, that would fit my personality even better. I remember my father trying to convince me to join him after he launched Covey Leadership Center.

I had just finished my MBA, and I was considering returning to real estate development. My father posed a great little statement that got me thinking. He said, "Stephen, that's great if you want to do real estate. Nothing wrong with that. It's exciting, it's fun; you're good at it. But do you want to spend your life building buildings or building souls?"

It struck me that—there's nothing wrong with building buildings, it's exciting work, but the chance to impact people, to really help people create and develop their own potential and to manifest this in their lives was very appealing. So I said, "You know what? I want to focus on building souls and building people, and the organizations in which they reside."

I made that move then and ran with that for many, many years, and helped build Covey Leadership Center into, as you mentioned, the largest leadership development company in the world. After the merger with Franklin Quest to form Franklin Covey, I stayed on with the new company, but then over time, decided I wanted to do some new things.

So I launched out on a number of different entrepreneurial ventures. Again, all of them were very exciting and interesting, very stimulating intellectually, but I recognized, after having experienced the work I'd been doing with Covey Leadership Center for so many years, that something was missing.

This time I knew it because I'd experienced it before. What was missing for me was that I needed to have all of my needs met. I wanted the work I was doing to matter, to make a difference— not just to make money and not just to have fun, and not just to develop my talents.

All of those things were very important to me, but I also wanted to make a difference in people's lives. So it's learning through living, that I've come around to understand, follow and run with what I consider to be my passions.

Chris: What's interesting in listening to you is that it sounds like you spent some time doing work you really did love at the Covey Leadership Center. But, then, you had to go off and spend time doing other things that perhaps were not quite as fulfilling in order to have the clarity to know what were truly your passions. Is that true?

Stephen: It's absolutely true. I spent some time [exploring options], even before Covey, but then I had this long period of time at Covey, and it was terrific. I was excited to try some new things, but you're exactly right. As I did those things, I found I definitely lacked some variety. I had to return to something with a spiritual dimension—some meaning, some purpose, some passion, my passion. I found that was vital. Having experienced the difference, I had to return to what I knew, so I'm back in the whole world of ideas and ways to help people.

Chris: Would you share with us, then, how you got from there to the speed of trust? That's really become a central theme of your work today hasn't it?

Stephen: It absolutely has. Over the last seventeen years, I've been involved heavily in this whole idea of releasing human potential, releasing talent, and in the process, I was a practitioner in it. I was not just someone talking about it. I actually was helping to build something and do something.

It became very clear to me that trust was the highest form of human motivation. It provided a motivation that was different in kind than anything else. I began to recognize that as I looked back at some of the early struggles we had at Covey Leadership Center.

Our issue was not whether or not we had a good idea in the marketplace. We did. We also had a lot of client appeal and attraction to what we were doing, but we were losing a lot of value by not really building an organization that had trust in all its relationships. We had trust with our key players, but we had not built an organization with the level of trust we needed yet.

I came across this great quote by Francis Fukuyama which really impacted me. It created a passion for this topic. The quote was this: "Widespread distrust in a society... imposes a kind of tax on all forms of economic activity, a tax that high-trust societies do not have to pay."

I began to think, "Well, not only is it in a society, but widespread distrust in an organization imposes a tax on everything." Widespread distrust in a relationship imposes a tax on every activity that high-trust organizations, high-trust relationships don't have to pay. While ours was not extremely low, because we had great people and we were doing good things, nonetheless, we felt there was a gap there. We were paying a tax. Any tax was too much and we were paying a tax.

So, I began to focus on how to eliminate this low trust tax and instead give the opposite of a tax, which is really a dividend. That was the whole notion of trust affecting everything else—everything around us in our organizations and our relationships. It began to be something I put more energy into, and saw it was something that was widely misunderstood in business, widely misunderstood in life, and it could have a profound impact.

So, it began as passion for ideas and for making a difference [and grew] into what I felt was a big idea that made a profound difference. Yet hardly anyone knew how to deal with it because it was seen as so soft and so fragile. I wanted to make it real and tangible. That's the whole idea of *The Speed of Trust*.

Chris: Could you give us examples of what you mean by a tax that occurs in low-trust environments?

Stephen: Sure. Let's take this tragedy that happened to the United States a few years ago, with this 9/11 activity, where a terrible terrorist act took place. After September 11th, trust in our entire air transportation system, the airline system in the United States, went down quite a bit, because people began to be worried about the safety of traveling.

It was both, "There are people out to get us" (Terrorists have an agenda), but also, "Is our system set up to catch them? Is it trustworthy? Is it capable of catching this?" So trust went down.

Trust always affects two measures every time. Whether it be low trust or high trust, it affects two measures. They are: speed and cost. When trust goes down, there's a tax. That tax is seen in slower speed—things take longer—and higher cost—things cost more.

Chris: Can you explain, in a little bit more detail, what you mean by the speed of trust?

Stephen: Well, here's an illustration. Warren Buffett, the CEO of Berkshire Hathaway, is well-known. He always writes a management letter every year with his annual report. His management letters are studied widely in business schools, elsewhere in the country and around the world.

A year ago, in his management letter, he talked about the big acquisition that his company, Berkshire Hathaway, did of a $23 billion company from Wal-Mart. This company was McLane Distribution Company—$23 billion in revenue. Now, Berkshire Hathaway is public, Wal-Mart is public, so these are two public companies.

They have all the requirements of the public marketplace; all the scrutiny, etc. But to make this deal happen, it took place in a two-hour meeting, and then twenty-nine days later, Wal-Mart had their money from Berkshire Hathaway for a $23 billion transaction. [Berkshire Hathaway] did no due diligence, and Warren Buffett said, "In essence, I trusted Wal-Mart, I trusted the people I worked with. I knew everything would be in exactly the order they said it would be, and it was." He said, "We did no due diligence," and in twenty-nine days they did this deal.

In most mergers of this size, we're talking several months, if not six, eight, ten, twelve months to close a deal like this, with armies and teams of accountants, CPAs, attorneys, etc, that come in and do all kinds of due diligence to verify, to validate. It costs a lot and it takes a lot of time.

But the idea of the speed of trust is literally, both speed in terms of actual time you can do things, but also speed as a metaphor, to mean benefits, results, dividends that are abundant—the fruits of high trust, the speed at which you're able to move, and the benefits produced.

In this case, a deal was done in twenty-nine days, start to finish, out of a two-hour meeting, because there was high trust in the relationship between the principals of these companies, and the fact they would not do anything wrong to the other. What an amazing ability to move, and with speed.

[In low trust relationships], the amount of time and energy that's wasted and spent on other agendas is extraordinary. It's characteristic of low trust, whereas high trust is the opposite. Things are open, they're on the table, there's no hidden agenda. It's transparent, and you're able to move with extraordinary speed. So it applies to the big boys and gals, and it also applies to basic, day-to-day relationships.

Chris: As we mentioned earlier, the title of this interview series is "The Passions of Real Life Legends," and in your father's newest book, *The 8th Habit*, he talks about four intelligences, which are key to an individual finding their own unique voice, or expressing their own unique, personal significance. Those are body, mind, heart and spirit.

I know that trust is wrapped up in these somehow, so could you share with us what is the role trust plays in allowing an individual to find and express their own unique voice, or to say it in different words, to live their own personal destiny?

Stephen: Great question. There are two key things trust impacts profoundly here, as it relates to our own uniqueness, our own missions and destinies. The first is this: we live today in an interdependent, inner-connected world. I'm not just talking about being wired and the fact it's a wired world and we're all connected that way. We are, but everything affects everything else.

It's an ecosystem, it's very interdependent, and there's very little that's truly isolated. It's a global economy, and changes taking place in India affect things in the United States and vice versa, and all over the world. In this interdependent world, it puts a premium on working with people, with multiple stakeholders.

By stakeholders, I mean those with a stake in your success and what you're doing, what you're all about. So these are customers, investors, suppliers, shareholders, employees, influencers, people you work with, people you want to influence. Relationships are at the heart of interdependence.

Trust is truly the key, the glue, that makes relationships work, for the reasons we've been discussing. It increases speed and decreases cost time and again. Relationships are at the heart of this interdependent world we're living in, and that's just the reality—we are living in this world.

So in most cases, as people are looking to live out and express their own unique voice, it generally is not isolated to them. It might be they want to impact, affect, work with, influence other people, in some way and fashion in their life, and the key to that interdependence is relationships. The key to relationships is trust, building relationships at the speed of trust, and carrying them out that way.

Chris: How does one go about building high-trust relationships? How do you go about being able to take advantage of that trust dividend, rather than having to pay the tax that comes with low trust?

Stephen: Once you make the case, people get the case. Do you know why they get it? Because they experience it, they have it in their own lives. Carl Rogers said, "That which is most personal is most general," so all of us have experienced relationships of low trust and relationships of high trust. All of us know that, so it applies across the board.

We get it. Once we frame it this way, then we say, "I get it. Help me now improve it." The process of building trust is an interesting one, but it begins with yourself, with what I call self trust, and with your own credibility, your own trustworthiness. If you think about it, it's hard to establish trust with others if you can't trust yourself. Trustworthiness is really the foundation upon which relationships or trust is built.

I call this self trust, building individual credibility. Basically, there are two dimensions to how trust works and how this individual credibility works. These dimensions are these: first, there's character, second, there's competence. Both are vital to building trust with others. Both are vital to building self trust.

Character is the one we understand the most as it relates to trust. When we think of trust, most of us put it in "softer" terms of character. It includes our integrity and the like. And that is true, it does. That's vital—the character component is vital because we need to have integrity to be trusted, to trust ourselves, as well as to have others trust us.

Also, we need to have competence. If you think about it, you don't trust someone if they're not competent to deliver results. You might trust their heart, their character, but you wouldn't trust them to get a job done.

My wife trusts me, I trust my wife. I care for her, I'm honest with her and she with me. She recently had to have some surgery, and you know what, Chris? As much as I trust her and she trusts me, she did not ask me to do the surgery, and it's obvious why not!

I'm not a doctor. I don't have any competence in the medical profession, and so she wouldn't trust me in that, and yet she would trust me to help raise a family with her. So, both character and competence are vital; and it just depends on what you need to accomplish, what you need to do.

Character is a constant and the competency needed is very task-oriented or job-oriented, very situation-oriented, but both are vital—character and competency.

Chris: Competency seems to grow, both from one's individual talents and from one's training. Character seems to be rooted much more deeply in our upbringing, in many different factors.

You've touched on this idea that trust within families is just as important as trust in the work environment. What is the role that family plays in this ability to have the kind of character that creates high-trust relationships, and in particular, I wonder if you could really make it personal, and share with our listeners what it was like to grow up in the Covey family? How did that contribute or not, to your own ability to understand and be able to build high-trust relationships?

Stephen: That's a great question. There's no question it's in our homes and our families where most people first learn about trust. We start with a basic, implicit understanding of it, and we extend trust rather easily, usually as young children.

In fact, right now, I have a two-year old, and I have an 18-year old. You talk about the two extremes—right in my own home. My two-year old trusts me implicitly, almost. If I ask her to jump into my arms, she will jump into my arms and I will catch her. We start learning trust at that age. We learn it and understand it.

With my 18-year old, I'm trying to teach him he needs to earn our trust to gain privileges. So if he's going to go out at night and there's a curfew, I expect him back at the curfew time, and if something holds him up, he needs to call. There's no question that we learn this trust in our homes, as well as in society, but our homes are probably our first experience with this, as we learn about it.

I was very blessed and fortunate to grow up in a home where both my father and mother were great models of this. Both teaching us integrity and teaching us the idea of making a difference and making a contribution in life, but also the way they interacted with us, really did build trust.

I'll give a brief example. A popular story, for those who have read my father's book, *The 7 Habits of Highly Effective People*, is the story of "Green and Clean." It's the story of my father training me (I was a young child at this time, about seven years old) how to take care of the yard, and how to make sure the yard was green and clean.

That was my job. I could do it however I wanted. My father recommended I might turn on the sprinklers because that would help, but he said, "If you want to use buckets and just pour water on the lawn, you can do that too." He taught me the idea was— you achieve results. The result here is I want a green yard, and clean. It was up to me on how to do it, but he gave me some good ideas on how to do it.

At the time, I was rather young. My father uses this story to talk about how he was teaching stewardship delegation and he was delegating to me results, and the responsibility to take care of that. And that is true. It was stewardship delegation. My father also talked about this in terms of being a win-win agreement, that he was teaching me that if I did this, here was my win, and here was his win, and it was a win-win agreement.

Do you know what, Chris? What I remember, because I was just seven years old, was that I felt trusted. I felt an extension of trust from my father to me, to take care of this yard. I was too young to care about money at the time. That didn't motivate me. What motivated me was I didn't want to let my father down.

I wanted to come through. I wanted to show I was capable and responsible for doing what he felt like I was doing. What he was giving me was this responsibility to take care of something. I felt trust. That motivated me. He extended it to me. It inspired me and built in me a sense of responsibility and stewardship and integrity that has stayed with me throughout my life and now I'm trying to pass it on to my children.

We clearly learn this in the home, both the character dimension of trust, but also how to extend trust, how to expand trust, and how to be a good model of this trust. The modeling is so important.

Example comes first, then relationship, then teaching, because example is seen, relationship is felt, teaching is heard. People tend not to hear until they see and feel, and that's what happened with me. I saw and I felt in my home. Then, that enabled me to hear, because of what I was seeing and feeling.

Chris: One of the things I'm hearing is that building trust is a process which takes place over time, with increasing levels of trusting involved at each stage. So, as we see that an individual or an organization is increasingly trustworthy, both in terms of character and competence, then we feel more confident to extend greater trust. So, it's a process that takes time, it sounds like?

Stephen: It is a process of taking time, of going through this, getting to know people better and their strengths better, and the task, and trying to match this up. There's the whole mind set you go into business and into life with, and that is, "Can I trust other people or not, and do I want to trust other people or not?"

People want to be trusted. It brings out the best in them. It's an extraordinary form of motivation. When people don't feel trusted, when they don't feel their boss trusts them, then it is a de-motivator and is discouraging. Then they are more apt to leave and go somewhere else, and do other things.

It doesn't bring out the best in them at all. It doesn't bring out their passion and their talents and creativity. It's very important to have a desire and intent to seek the trust of other people. You just don't want to get ahead of yourself with extending too much trust beyond their competence or their character.

Business is better by releasing people and their talents and capabilities. I remember Robert Galvin, Jr., the CEO of Motorola, who took over from his father. He did a great job and he said he was asked this question: "People ask me how I had the interest and the zeal to hang in there and do what I've done. I say, 'Because my father treated me with very stern discipline. He trusted me. I'm stuck. I've got to see the trust through. He trusted me. I trust other people, and they do the job.'"

So, the whole idea was, trust is a great form of motivation—

of releasing talent, energy, passion—of releasing your own energy and passion by being trusted and also by extending trust to other people. You just want to make sure you do it with wisdom and understanding character and competence. You've got to match them up. What's the competence needed to perform the task at hand?

Chris: I know you do a lot of work with organizations, and we've talked about the role family plays. What's the relationship between families and work team environments? How does trust or the lack thereof that one grows up with, express itself in a work team environment?

Stephen: You see it in work environments all over. In fact, again, the data is overwhelming that we actually have a crisis of trust in organizational life. Watson Wyatt did a survey which showed that only 39 percent of employees trusted their senior leaders. If you don't trust the people running your company...

We can write the program and we can create our own script. We can build relationships of trust, build teams of trust and cultures of trust. I mentioned, when I talked about how you go about doing this, the need is to first start with yourself and be credible, to focus on your character, your competence first.

Also this: Learn how to interact in ways that build the trust within your relationship, and learn how to avoid the ways that destroy it. Let me give just two simple examples that everyone can apply today, tonight, or tomorrow. Here are two ways you can immediately begin to increase trust in a relationship.

The first is to create more transparency in any given relationship. By transparency, I mean openness. It means to tell the truth in a way that other people can validate, can verify. The opposite of transparency is having a hidden agenda because then you're not open. There you've got something hidden, and in most cases, people sense it; they feel it. They don't know what it is, but they distrust what you're doing because they question what your real agenda or motive is.

Instead, be transparent; be open. "Here's what I'm trying to do. Here's why."

Companies that do this, leaders that do this, experience far greater results. Individuals who do this in relationships get better results because it opens things up, and they realize, "Here's your agenda. Your agenda is on the table." It's open, it's clear.

Recently, there's been a big challenge with some charities, [where people are asking] "What are you using your money for?" If people are going to donate money to charities, you can't lose that trust. The best way to keep it is to become transparent: open up your books, open up what you're doing with the money.

If people are questioning what you're doing, open it up. Make sure you're worthy of that by doing the right things with the money. But, if trust is low, people don't trust what they can't see. Instead, let them see it, open it up. I know a lot of companies have opened up their financial books and let people see the financials because the very process of doing that is a great demonstration of trust. You need to apply this in your own situation. If you're trying to build trust in a particular relationship ask, "How can I be more open, more transparent so others can see what I'm really trying to do—my intent, my motive?"

In the very process of doing that, you challenge yourself because maybe you're not being open. Maybe you do have a hidden agenda. If you do, you're not going to be building trust. People will sense it. Instead, be open, be clear, be transparent, and you'll be amazed at the immediate impact it can have.

Let me give you the second thing. You can take issues head on. Confront reality, take these issues head on, even things that are so-called "un-discussable," because so often what happens is we skirt issues. We avoid them, we run from them, especially for a leader within a company or within a team.

If there are things everyone's talking about, but we're not talking about it as a team, it's the un-discussable. Yet everyone discusses it behind the scenes. Ignoring it only decreases trust because it signifies one of two things: either you're not open and honest with people, which is not being transparent, or you're clueless, you don't understand.

That's not good either. So which is it? Both are bad. So, instead of ignoring it and skirting it, take it head on, tee it up. Say, "I understand we've got this issue. Let's discuss this," because it's being discussed anyway with or without you. Why not have it be with you?

I had this situation, after the merger of Franklin and Covey. We had a group we were really struggling with building trust. All mergers are tough; they struggle with trust issues, and we did too. Here I was, the president of this unit, trying to build trust. I had a one-hour speech with a team of consultants.

We were supposed to talk about strategy. You know what? I could see and sense no one really wanted to talk about strategy. They wanted to talk about a whole host of merger issues that were dividing the culture and dividing us from bringing our companies together.

I decided, you know, I can talk about strategy, play it safe, and probably get nowhere. Or, I could really open it up and say, "What would you really like to talk about?" knowing they wanted to talk about these things, and then make it safe for them by bringing some of these issues up myself.

So, I did that. I opened it up and said, "I sense from private conversations some of you would really like to talk about what's our process of integrating these companies. Who's making the decisions? Who's philosophy is winning out? How are we going about doing this? Which physical facilities are we going to keep and not? Is that right?"

Everyone said, "Yeah! We really would like to talk about

that." Then, they opened up and they began to ask real tough questions. Rather than skirt them, I took them head on. The net effect was I had people afterwards say to me, "You know what? We built more trust in one day than we had in the prior year. I appreciate your being open and honest and taking these issues head on."

I didn't have answers for everything, and I'm not giving myself as a great model of this. I struggled too, but I've learned creating transparency and confronting reality are two quick, easy ways any of us can increase the trust in relationships and with our teams and organizations.

Chris: This has been such a pleasure, and I have to say, I could go on talking to you for a long time. We're coming close to the end of our time together. At Healthy, Wealthy, nWise, Stephen, we believe strongly in the power of intention to manifest outcomes. What is your biggest current project, and what intention would you like us, here at Healthy, Wealthy, nWise, along with our readers, to hold for you?

Stephen: I'm excited about this work I'm doing on trust, and the biggest project is really this: I'm building what I call a "trust practice." The whole idea is to focus on helping individuals and organizations build trust, create trust, grow trust with all stakeholders they interact with, in order to improve business results and their own personal results in their lives.

Part of this includes a book that will be coming out focusing on business at the speed of trust, and will probably be called, *The Speed of Trust*. It's much more than just business, it's relationships and so much more—leadership at the speed of trust.

This has excited me. I'm taking on a topic that has been very much misunderstood and almost even maligned by some. There are so many myths around trust. It's seen as soft, it's seen as slow, as nebulous. I saw something this week that said, "Can you teach trust?"

I want to emphatically answer: Absolutely! Trust can be taught, it can be learned, it can be implemented, it can be grown, it can be measured, it can be applied in an organization, and it can and should be an explicit objective of every relationship, of every organization. It's there whether you're aware of it or not. Either you have trust or you don't.

If you have it, you'll get a dividend. It will pay results to you in countless ways. You'll see it in speed and cost. If trust is low, you're also paying a price; you're paying this tax that will be manifest in speed and cost, and is happening whether you believe it or buy it.

It's inevitable that low trust means low speed, high cost. It happens throughout, so I'm trying to show how you can measure this. You can quantify this, and you can then do something about it. I'm making the case, and then I'm showing what you can do about it, both individually and within companies, to increase trust and to get the great fruits, the great dividends, and the great speed of trust within companies and also within relationships.

So that's my big objective, building this trust practice, helping individuals and organizations practice trust and see the great dividends that come from doing it.

I think the final thought or idea I'd leave with your readers is simply this: I predict the ability to create, grow, extend and restore trust with all stakeholders will become the key leadership competency of the 21st century. And I mean that seriously—more than strategy, more than vision, more than all these different things.

The reason I say that—it's a pretty bold prediction to say it's going to be the key leadership competency, the ability to create, grow, extend and restore trust with all stakeholders—is we're in a knowledge worker economy, where relationships are the key. Low trust is everywhere in our society and our organizations, it's all around us.

There's an extraordinary high cost of this low trust, that we see manifest in both speed and cost, and trust affects everything else we do. It affects our strategy, our execution, our innovation, our communication. Every dimension in a company, in a relationship, is affected by trust, its presence or absence.

Therefore, as we increase the trust in our organizations and our relationships, we then experience this multiplicative effect, this multiplier that increases rather than taxes what we're doing. It increases the communication rather than taxes it. It increases our ability to execute rather than discounting our ability to execute, and it affects every dimension, every aspect of this.

So it's an exciting thing to be a part of. There are many things we could immediately do to impact it, and I'm delighted to have this opportunity to talk with your listeners about this vital and business-critical topic.

Chris: It is vital. Stephen, thank you so much for being with us. It is a great honor and privilege to be able to spend this time with you. I want to repeat, for all of our readers, the homework you gave them because I want to make it very specific.

You have suggested we can begin creating more trusting relationships right now, tonight or tomorrow. So, for all of our readers, my challenge to each of us is to pick one person in the next day or two and choose to be more transparent.

Choose to be open in a situation that maybe you haven't been in the past. Do it with someone who you already have a close relationship with so it's not too scary. Choose a situation to create more transparency.

Secondly, Stephen suggested taking an issue which you ordinarily wouldn't discuss with someone straight on. Maybe it's one of those un-discussable issues Stephen described.

Choose to bring it out for discussion, and see what the results are. Did I state that clearly enough, Stephen?

Stephen: Absolutely. These are two things you could do in any relationship right away, using your judgment as to how best to apply it. Here's a third: make a commitment and keep it. Make a commitment with another person and keep it, and make another one and keep it.

You'll build trust with yourself because you make commitments and keep them, but you build trust with others. See, when you make a commitment, you build hope. When you keep a commitment, you build trust. So, making and keeping commitments is another immediate way to start to increase trust in a relationship.

To learn more about the work of Stephen M. R. Covey, visit:
http://www.coveylink.com

What were the key lessons from this interview about living your passion?

1. When life is not aligned with our passions, it feels like something is missing.

2. Sometimes even when we discover our passions, we may have to do something else for a while to have the contrast which will allow us to realize what's really most important to us.

3. Trust is the highest form of human motivation.

4. Distrust imposes a tax. High trust relationships and organizations enjoy a dividend.

5. Trust always affects two measures: speed and cost. When trust goes down, things take longer and cost more. When trust goes up, things happen faster and at a lower cost.

6. As we seek to live our passions and fulfill our destiny, we are not isolated. Relationships are key to our ability to fulfill our personal destiny. Trust is fundamental to any relationship.

7. The process of building trust begins with yourself, with your own credibility, your own trustworthiness. It's hard to establish trust with others if you can't trust yourself.

8. There are two dimensions to building trust: character and competence. Both are vital to building trust.

9. When we extend trust, we give others the opportunity to prove themselves trustworthy.

10. Modeling trust by example comes first, then building trust in relationships, then teaching trust.

11. Building trust takes place over time, with increasing levels of trusting at each stage in a relationship.

12. When people feel trusted, it brings out the best in them.

13. It's important to seek to build trust with others. Just don't get ahead of yourself with extending too much trust beyond the other's character and/or competence.

14. Two ways anyone can apply to increase trust in a relationship: create more transparency; and take issues head on.

15. Trust should be an explicit objective of every relationship and every organization.

16. The ability to create, grow, extend and restore trust with all stakeholders will become the key leadership competency of the 21st century.

Homework:

- Pick one person and choose to be more transparent with them;

- Select an issue with someone you're close to which you ordinarily wouldn't discuss head on, and choose to bring it out for discussion; and

- Make a commitment with another person and keep it, then make another one and keep it.

How will you use these points in your own life starting now?

You can be part of the live teleaudience, absolutely FREE, when Healthy Wealthy nWise conducts interviews with amazing people like the one you just read. Go to:

http://www.healthywealthynwise.com/interview

There you can quickly and easily sign up to receive reminders on all of the incredible upcoming calls.

12

DEBBIE FORD

RESIGNING AS
GENERAL MANAGER OF THE UNIVERSE

By: Janet Attwood and Gay Hendricks

Debbie Ford is the #1 New York Times *best-selling author of* The Dark Side of the Light Chasers: Reclaiming Your Power, Creativity, Brilliance and Dreams *and an internationally recognized expert in the field of personal transformation and human potential.*

She has been a guest many times on Oprah *and* Good Morning America *as well as the* Roseanne *show,* FOX News *and* WNBC. *Debbie has also been featured in* O magazine, Self magazine, USA Today, *the* Los Angeles Times *and many others.*

Debbie is sought after as a life coach. People like Alanis Morissette, Bonnie Raitt, Donna Karan and many others have benefited from her guidance. She is the founder of the Ford Institute for Integrative Coaching at JFK University, a personal development organization that

*provides professional training for individuals who are committed to lead-
ing extraordinary lives. Her teachings and revolutionary inner processes have made her a renowned coach, transformational speaker and seminar leader.*

*This interview was conducted by Gay Hendricks. Gay and his wife
Katie are co-founders and directors of the Hendricks Institute which
teaches core skills for conscious living (www.hendricks.com). Over the
past 30 years, Gay and Katie have helped thousands of people open to
more creativity, love, joy and vitality through the power of conscious living and whole-person learning.*

Gay: It is our privilege and honor to have Debbie as our guest
this evening, and one of the things I want to say is I think this
woman is a national/international treasure. Debbie, thank you for
joining us.

Debbie: Thank you for having me.

Gay: What role, Debbie, did your passions, the things that
are most important to you, play in the emergence of your books?

Debbie: Well, really they've sparked everything, and even
today, I feel my passion is to teach people to love themselves completely. Not just love the part of themselves that is loveable, like
the charming, sweet, smart part, but to love all of themselves,
including their darkness.

I wrote my first book out of this passion to share that God did
create us as amazing individuals, and we have this similar blue-
print within all of us. We all are everything; the good and the bad,
the light and the dark, the sweet and the sour, the fearful and the
courageous.

The Dark Side of the Light Chasers was birthed out of that passion to show people we all have these dark parts. We all have dark
spots, parts of ourselves we feel ashamed of, scared of, embarrassed

by. We can't wish those parts away, but we can learn to integrate them and love even those parts of ourselves.

That passion exists probably more in me today, Gay. I am more fascinated by what I do today than when I started. That still drives me to do everything I do.

Gay: Well, I think that's a sign, Debbie, that you're really on the right track as far as your work is concerned, because I know when I am around people like yourself that are really passionate, what it speaks to is that the work you are doing and the work you are teaching has an intrinsic validity to it and an integrity to it, out of which more and more passion comes.

Congratulations on getting a book to the top of the *New York Times* best seller list. How did that happen?

Debbie: It was one of those magical moments. I always try to teach people now that there is only so much you can effort into the world. I remember when *The Dark Side of the Light Chasers* first came out I was sure, like many people are who write, that it would go to the top of the list and I was going to get on Oprah and everything was going to be great and easy.

I passionately went out in the world and spoke to three people or seven people or fifteen, whoever would listen to me and it really took years for all the pieces to fit together. I had great people giving Oprah my book, but still nobody called. Now I look back and say some things are just meant to be, and they're going to happen when they are meant to be. There is only so much you can accomplish by effort.

I know you're an author so you understand the "Oprah desire" for authors because it propels your work out into the world. It was at a time when I was surrendering and had given up that dream and said, "Okay, what do I have to do to get my work out into the world? I'll do anything." I was working day and night to do whatever I had to do.

Then, of course, a few things happened. I met Cheryl Richardson, who was on Oprah all the time at that point, and she said to me, "Wow! Your work is so important. What can I do to support you? Why haven't you been on Oprah?" It was interesting because she had me look at why I hadn't gotten my work out in the world the way I wanted to, and what I saw was that I was scared I would just become overwhelmed because I was already overwhelmed with my task.

The moment of truth of seeing I was the one that had the blocks up, I was the one that was really scared and saying, "I can't take more than I have," reminded me I didn't really need to do anything, if I would just surrender, God, or my spirit, would take care of me. When we have done all we can do, remarkable things happen when we surrender.

I did that and literally three days later I got called to do the Oprah show. I did three shows and then they re-aired all three of them. Within a couple of months my books—and shadow work—went out in the world.

Gay: That's so remarkable. Ours was almost an identical experience. We kind of beat our brains out with our book, *Conscious Loving,* to get on Oprah for the first year it was out in hardback. The Persian Gulf War was going on and so it didn't happen. Suddenly, a year later, when the paperback came out, literally one night we were sitting in our living room working with six couples, and two days later we were working with ten million people on Oprah.

You never know how those kinds of things are going to happen, but one thing I hear you speaking to, which I really appreciate, Debbie, is that you're open to both the conscious manifestation and also open to letting things happen in magical ways.

Debbie: Yes, and I think that's the hardest part. So much of what I know, Gay, just so you know, is because of you and [your wife] Katie, who are both brilliant teachers. So much of the human desire is to make it happen and to think you can do everything, that you are the driver.

When you give up being the driver, there is a bigger driver that is going to do a much better job than you. It's about remembering to ask yourself, 'What can I do today to resign as general manager of the universe so I can allow what I am supposed to be doing?'

I fell in love with a prayer when I was recovering from drug addiction twenty-five years ago. It was in the *Alcoholics Anonymous Big Book*, which was "I offer myself to thee to build with me and do with me as thy will. Relieve me of the bondage of self so I may better do thy will."

I'm sure I'm not saying it right, but that phrase "to relieve me of the bondage of self," I love that. I used to be on my hands and knees every day for five years; my prayer was to just use me, relieve me of what I think I should be doing and allow the universe to use me for some greater cause. I feel like today I am being used for that greater cause and I love it.

Gay: That's a beautiful, beautiful message. I don't think we can hear it too often, and I also love that phrase "resigning as general manager of the universe."

Debbie: Especially when it comes to getting a book on the New York Times list; you can't make it happen. If it's going to happen, it's because there are a lot of things lined up to make it happen. How are you going to love yourself even if it doesn't happen?

Gay: Yes, exactly. I was leafing through this wonderful new book of yours, *The Best Year of Your Life*. How about telling us a little bit about that, and then I have a couple of very specific questions to ask you about how that book came to be. Why don't you tell everybody about that?

Debbie: Well, *The Best Year of Your Life* is really about becoming the person you desire to be at the end of the year. Not that you have to change your goals, because, yes, I have had many years where I have attained everything I ever wanted in the material world, but was left feeling empty inside.

The years where I have worked on my inner world and have had that balance between inner and outer; at the end of the year, if I have made good choices, if I have allowed myself to evolve, and if I've surrendered and I love who I am, then nothing else really matters. That is what I see from teaching and being a trainer and training coaches, when you are loving your life, magic happens.

The Best Year of Your Life, ultimately, even though it's subtitled, "Dream it, Plan it and Live it," and does give people those tools on how to make things happen in the outer world, really, its point is, "Who do I have to be in the inner world to create effortlessly and easily with joy, the things which will nourish me in the outer world?"

Maybe I don't even know what they are, because oftentimes, the things we think we want aren't exactly what will bring us happiness.

Gay: That really speaks to one of the questions I wanted to ask you about *The Best Year of Your Life*. One of the things which impresses me about [your book] is that it is so much about balance, about creating more openness in the inner world at the same time as you're manifesting your heart's desires in the outer world.

How are you able to practice the principles in the book, with the pressures and the busyness of your life?

Debbie: I'd like to say I am a master at it, but you know they say you write what you need to learn. It's been a really hard lesson and I think that's why I write about it so much. The great news is I have a ten-year old I love and love to be with. That really has me stay at home where before I used to be on the road and I could drag him around. The last four years he doesn't want to go anywhere with me. He doesn't even want to skip school!

I go back and forth between the outer and the inner and taking time to do some yoga or meditate or just send some love. My work is all about having people go inside to find the answers, and I lead so many training calls where I'm leading meditations, and I always do the work myself. That, of course, gives me a balance I could never get anywhere else if I wasn't doing that, because it's really part of my work.

Gay: If people were going to take away a central idea of one practical step they could do to create the best year of their life, what's something they could do?

Debbie: Well, my favorite chapter, I think, is the chapter on fantasy. That chapter busts the fantasy of that "one day" you're waiting for: when I finally get on Oprah, when I finally finish my movie, when my husband finally starts treating me this way, when my child goes to college, when I finally have enough money. That "one day" fantasy, I feel, is what robs people of having the best year; creating it and being responsible for it, right here and now.

There is nobody in the world who can make your life great but you. For example, I share in the book about when *Dark Side* made number one. That had been my "one day" fantasy. Well, after my book rose to number one, I was depressed. Actually, I never even enjoyed it because I was so busy, and I didn't know what it meant to be number one on the New York Times list, to tell you the truth.

I remember screaming and then that was it. I forgot about the whole thing; I didn't understand it at the time. But afterwards, I went into a very dark time.

I was leading a seminar, a Shadow Process at the Chopra Center, and Deepak and somebody else came over to congratulate me, and they were like, "Well, how are you doing?" I said, "To be honest with you, I'm not doing that great, and I feel really sad."

I realized I was searching for this fantasy and thought when I got there, I would suddenly feel like I mattered.

Gay: Your fantasy that [this] was the one that was going to do it for you.

Debbie: Exactly. Then there was no fantasy and I didn't know how to make myself matter to me. I didn't really know how to acknowledge myself, and I realized after that, Gay, I could just call Aunt Pearl. She would tell me I mattered; or my sister Arielle, she would tell me I mattered. I needed to take that back, take responsibility and tell myself why I mattered. I was going too fast to matter in my own life.

When I started doing that, I distinguished the feeling and what I needed and started waking up every day saying, "What could I do to feel like I matter, or feel important or feel worthy today?" I just did it for six months and at the end, I felt tremendous. All of a sudden, there was nothing out there to chase.

If you're looking for admiration or for love or to feel successful, ask yourself, how will you feel when you're successful? Then start feeling that way now. You're not going to find it outside of yourself.

I know you know this from working with a lot of people who are celebrities, or who have a lot of money; almost all of them go through this. Like, "Oh my God! I finally got where I wanted to go and I don't feel like I'm supposed to feel."

Gay: Why do you think it is so many of us sabotage ourselves when we're trying to achieve our goals and dreams, that we somehow get in our own way and we even do that more than once? We become serial saboteurs, I guess you might say. Why do you think that is?

Debbie: Well, the first thing that comes to me is a quote my friends Paul and Layne Cutright once said, "The guilty seek punishment." I feel, especially since I do so much shadow work, most people hold a lot of grudges and resentments, not only towards other people, but towards themselves.

That unforgiving nature most humans have—the internal world where we're beating ourselves up and the external world is always a mirror of our internal world. People internally are beating themselves up and then all of a sudden they wonder why they're doing things in the outer world to beat themselves up. It's just a way to affirm those internal messages most of us have that we're not good enough or we'll never get what we want, or whatever our programming is.

To stop sabotaging ourselves, we begin by forgiving ourselves, for being part of the human race, with flaws, imperfections, misbehaving, and sometimes making wrong choices. We have to forgive ourselves for being flawed, for being imperfect, for not doing it right, for not always behaving, for making choices that are not in our highest and best interests.

The foundation of all my long-term training is self-forgiveness because what I know is if you can forgive yourself internally and have compassion and openheartedness toward that sweet, vulnerable child who lives inside of you, then you will create those kinds of magical moments in the outer world. The outer world will reflect that self-love and you won't want to sabotage yourself.

You'll be careful who you hang around and what you say you're going to do, because you become precious to yourself.

Gay: One of the most important parts of that is something you have addressed a lot in your work. I think it's probably the most important thing people can do at a certain stage of their lives, and that is handle projection. You talk a lot about projection and it is such an important thing. I wonder if you could talk about what you mean by it and how you work with projection.

Debbie: I would love to because that is my passion. Projection is transferring either good or bad qualities we see in ourselves onto someone else. There is only one person in the world we can't see if we have sight, only one, and that person is our self.

God created us so magically. Just like the body functions so magically when it's working, so does our psyche. We are designed in a way where the only way we can see ourselves is to look "out there" and to look at other people. If I want to know my light side, my best self, all I have to do is look in the outer world and look for who I love, who turns me on, who excites me and distinguish the qualities I am seeing in them, and in doing that I will find the best expression of myself.

The same is true for my darkness. I can't see my own darkness, even though I think I can. If I look out there and I see people who are angry, or insensitive, or rude, or mean, again I'm seeing myself. I'm seeing the disowned parts of myself.

Ken Wilber uses that expression. How do you know something's a projection? He says, "When we are informed by somebody else." When we receive someone else's behavior simply as information, it's probably not a projection. When we react, get upset, blame, accuse, or when we put others on a pedestal, we are projecting our own feelings about our self onto someone else.

If we are affected in any way, like pointing our finger, blaming, going off like "that shouldn't be like that" or "they're bad" or "they're wrong", we're seeing a part of ourselves we don't embrace and we don't own.

People do it with their light, with teachers. I always tell people, "Don't do it to me. I don't need your light. I have my own." But people say "Oh! You're so brilliant, or you're so articulate." No, you're just seeing your own brilliance, or your own way of articulating inside of me, your own creative self. If we could all take ourselves back from other people, then everybody becomes our peer. Then we have the power to say, "Wow!"

Gay: That's wonderful. One of the things we say in our work, how you know you're projecting is to listen to yourself complain. Anything you hear yourself complain about three or more times is sure to be a projection.

Yes, the power of it is—I know you've spoken about this so much in your books—you get this incredible creative power from owning your projections. The moment you reach out and embrace them with love, you really harness that power and can ride it to a different level in your life.

Debbie: I love that. When we own our dark projections, we gain freedom.

Gay: Yes, and that beautiful phrase you used, "standing in your power," that's really what it's all about. Talk about what you mean by standing in your power and the gift of doing that.

Debbie: Standing in your power is being aligned with the highest parts of yourself, and knowing both your humanity and your divinity. Even though we are living a human experience, we are divine beings. When I'm standing in my power, I'm being true to myself, to my highest self, and I'm embracing all of myself, even my lowest self.

How do you know you're standing in your power? You're empowered; you don't want for anything. You're not wishing, comparing yourself to other people. You're happy to be who you are. We are designed that way. That's why I love leading transformational [workshops]. People think I'm a genius, but really I don't have to do anything. All I have to do is support people in getting reconnected with their whole self—light and dark aspects included, and they will stand in their power. They'll be awed and wowed by their own self. We all have that ability.

I love the analogy that we're like these great pieces of art. A sculptor would look at a piece of stone, and they can see the magnificence in it.

They know what the creation is, so all they have to do is chisel away anything that's not that, and there they are. They have a masterpiece.

That's all we have to do. We don't have to become anything, we already are everything we ever wanted to be, and we just have to chisel away anything that is distracting us or blocking us from seeing that self. Then, voila—we wind up in our power naturally. Is it work? It is, right, Gay? It's work....

That's what's so interesting about love. I know you teach this, so you know better than anybody, that the person you love one minute, you can hate the next. All it is, is projection. If people understood that projection is a trance—you go into a trance when you've disowned parts of yourself, energetically.

You're sure the other person is that way. But the power comes from being willing to do our own work....

Gay: That's what I always tell my students too. Whenever somebody criticizes you, finds fault or accuses you, the fastest thing you can do to get the lesson of it is to cheerfully agree with it. Just say, "Yes, that's part of me too!"

Debbie: I have to tell you my Beau story. My son Beau is 10 years old; I pick him up from school less than a week ago. He's never used this language; he says, "Mommy, I'm using one of your life lessons." I've never heard him say 'life lessons.' I'm like, "Oh, really, Beau? What are you using?"

He said, "Today, so-and-so called me stupid."

I said, "Oh, really?"

Beau said, "Yes, and I said, 'Yes, I'm stupid!'" Then the kid said, "Hey, everybody, Beau just called himself stupid!" Beau looked at him and said, "So, what's the point?" He said, "Then the kid went away."

Gay: That has been one of the most wonderful quotes to come out of this conversation to me. I'm going to quote Beau: "I'm stupid, so what's the point?"

Debbie: Yes, like what is the problem with that? I love that. When we are loving ourselves, we don't need to fight with others when they don't like us, or don't treat us well. People are going to hate us, people are going to try to block us, people aren't always going to give us what we want or meet our expectations, and we can just surrender.

Gay: That's beautiful. That's one thing I really got a lot of value out of in this conversation. Another thing which I always like to hear about and got a lot of value out of was your emphasis on projection, when you see things out there in the world that you find yourself complaining about or obsessing about, or looking at critically or judgmentally—to benignly, lovingly bring that attention back to yourself and say, "What part of me is that reflecting?" I really appreciate you bringing projection out into the world for us in such an eloquent way.

Debbie: It is my passion, so you can count on me to do it until the day they have to put me under. I feel like I got it in such a huge way, and what a great gift to give yourself, to take back your projections, not just your negative ones but your positive ones as well.

Gay: I also appreciate and want to salute that incredible, passionate attention you give to the shadow, to making sure we acknowledge and own all those things about ourselves we sometimes tend to criticize; to open our embrace to that too, to open your embrace of your inner world at the same time as you make progress in the outer world.

Debbie: Thank you, Gay. You are one of my inspirations, so I am honored and thrilled to have you interview me and to be a part of this community.

Gay: Thank you so much for joining us today. I'd like to turn things back over to Janet.

Janet: Thank you both so much. What an honor to be able to sit here and absorb the depth of wisdom that you both have. I think it's so profound, Debbie and Gay, that here I am in India, meeting all kinds of masters and gurus for my current project, and I'm still sitting at the feet of two masters this morning, so thank you.

All I continue to absorb in India, as I've been here over the past year off and on, is the knowledge that to truly be happy, one has to go within and know yourself. Both of you clearly are masters of that, so thank you so much.

For all of our listeners, be sure to find out how to create the best year of your life by getting a copy of Debbie's latest book, *The Best Year of Your Life*, at www.thebestyearofyourlife.com.

I have a question for all of you. Is there any reason why this shouldn't be your best year ever?

We all know the answer is: absolutely not. Debbie's book will show you how to dream it, plan it and live it. Go to her website and begin creating the best year you've ever had.

To learn more about the work of Debbie Ford, visit:
www.debbieford.com and www.bestyearofyourlife.com

What were the key lessons from this interview about living your passion?

1. We all have dark aspects, parts of ourselves we feel ashamed of, scared of, embarrassed by. We can't wish those parts away, but we can learn to integrate them and love even those parts of ourselves.

2. Some things are meant to be, and they're going to happen when they are meant to be. There is only so much you can accomplish through effort.

3. When we have done all we can do, remarkable things happen when we surrender. When you give up being the driver, there is a bigger driver that is going to do a much better job than you.

4. Who do I have to be in my inner world to create effortlessly and easily with joy, the things that will nourish me in the outer world?

5. If you're looking for admiration or for love or to feel successful, ask yourself, how will you feel when you're successful? Then start feeling that way now. You're not going to find it outside of yourself.

6. To stop sabotaging ourselves, we begin by forgiving ourselves, for being part of the human race, with flaws, imperfections, misbehaving, and sometimes making wrong choices.

7. Projection is transferring either good or bad qualities we see in ourselves onto someone else.

8. When we receive someone else's behavior simply as information, it's probably not a projection. When we react, get upset, blame, accuse, or when we put others on a

pedestal, we are projecting our disowned thoughts, feelings and beliefs about our self onto someone else.

9. When we own our projections, we gain freedom.

10. Standing in your power is being aligned with the highest parts of yourself and knowing both your humanity and your divinity.

11. You know you are standing in your power when you feel empowered, you don't want for anything.

12. When we are loving ourselves, we don't need to fight with others when they don't like us, or don't treat us well, or block us.

How will you use these points in your own life starting now?

You can be part of the live teleaudience, absolutely FREE, when Healthy Wealthy nWise conducts interviews with amazing people like the one you just read. Go to:

http://www.healthywealthynwise.com/interview

There you can quickly and easily sign up to receive reminders on all of the incredible upcoming calls.

13

DR. JOHN HAGELIN

UNITED AT OUR CORE

By: Chris Attwood

Dr. John Hagelin *is a world authority in the area of unified quantum field theories. His scientific contributions in the fields of particle physics and cosmology include some of the most cited references in the physical sciences.*

He is co-developer of what is now considered the leading contender for a grand unified field theory, known as Supersymmetric Flipped SU(5). Dr. Hagelin is unique among particle theorists in his dedicated efforts to apply the latest scientific understanding of natural law for the benefit of the individual and society.

As director of the Institute of Science, Technology and Public Policy, a progressive policy think tank, Dr. Hagelin has successfully headed a nationwide effort to identify, scientifically verify and promote cost-effective solutions to critical social problems in the fields of crime, health care, education, economy, energy and the environment.

In recognition of his outstanding achievements, Dr. Hagelin was named winner of the prestigious Kilby Award, which honors scientists who have made major contributions to society through their applied research in the fields of science and technology. The award recognized Dr. Hagelin as a scientist in the tradition of Einstein, Genes, Bohr, and Edington.

As the 2000 presidential candidate of the Natural Law Party, Dr. Hagelin, along with hundreds of NLP candidates in all fifty states, drew millions of votes for his scientifically proven, forward-looking, sustainable solutions to America's pressing social, economic and environmental problems. He has recently founded the US Peace Government, a complementary government, dedicated to prevention-oriented administration.

Dr. Hagelin has appeared many times on ABC's Nightline *and* Politically Incorrect, NBC's Meet the Press, CNN's Larry King Live *and* Inside Politics, CNBC's Hardball with Chris Matthews, C-SPAN's Washington Journal, *and others. He's featured in the five time award-winning film* What the #@%$ (Bleep) Do We Know, *and he has been regularly featured in the* Washington Post, the New York Times, the Wall Street Journal, USA Today, the Los Angeles Times, the San Francisco Chronicle, *and now,* Healthy Wealthy nWise.

Chris: John, as a legend in the field of quantum physics as well as politics, we asked you to write down at least ten things that, if you had them completely fulfilled, would make your life ideal.

Would you share those with us?

Dr. Hagelin: Yes, Chris, I'll be happy to. The most important key to success and happiness in my life is experiencing unbounded awareness, the field of pure spirituality within, and identifying my awareness with the unified field—the universal intelligence that governs the universe. This brings immediate expansion, joy, pure creativity, and total support of nature for health and success and happiness in life.

If I had to give number two, I would say more of the above. I'm really blessed with a program that brings immediate expansion, immediate bliss, and immediate contact with the infinite. I'm fortunate to be a teacher of the Transcendental Meditation® program as taught by Maharishi Mahesh Yogi, which is the world's most widely practiced, widely researched and broadly prescribed technology for the full development of human potential.

Three, I need purposeful activity that brings evolution to humankind, activity that alleviates global problems and suffering, and promotes peace in the world. I need to see tangible results, tangible success in this and all my projects. I'm passionate about peace, about ending this terrible legacy of human cruelty and warfare, as well as the deep ignorance that permits such life-afflicting behavior.

I'm passionate about education, especially education for enlightenment, a new paradigm of education that involves full human potential that develops the total brain. Modern education is really a travesty in that it develops a mere sliver of one's brain potential, and as a result, it deprives a human being of his or her natural capability of living enlightenment.

I am a born teacher and I need to teach. Karmically, the teacher always gains more than he gives. The way to understand anything most profoundly is to explain it to someone else, and that's the experience of every teacher.

I teach graduate courses in unified quantum field theories. The way to really own the material is to impart that understanding to someone else, and somehow, magically almost, the material organizes itself more clearly and profoundly for the teacher.

I love being with people who are evolving, who share this natural joy of life, and especially those who are enlightened, established in higher states of consciousness. The activities of such people are naturally evolutionary, life-giving, bliss-bestowing.

I love speaking to large audiences, and the medium of live television, probably because it leverages one's impact and ability to reach large numbers of people and thus make a difference. I love art and music and being surrounded by inspiration and beauty.

I love living in a dwelling built in accord with natural law, a dwelling designed for maximum, life-supporting, life-nourishing influence. Maharishi's Sthapatya Vedic architecture, which is more ancient and more complete than Feng Shui, is a tremendous blessing and a formula for success in itself.

Chris: Wow, that's quite a list. John, what roles have the things you're passionate about played in your life?

Dr. Hagelin: Well, I think for me to address the question, we have to spend a little time understanding what passion is. For me, to understand what passion is gets to the core nature of life, the very purpose of life, which is to progress and to evolve and grow toward fulfillment.

If we're progressing and evolving, then we experience joy, energy, vitality, health. Those activities through which we grow—through which we expand in knowledge, expand in power, expand in fulfillment—it's that type of activity that brings us joy. This is the joy born of expansion, born of progress, born of evolution.

If I'm passionate about something or you're passionate about something, it's because that something brings joy to us, nourishment to us—that activity is a path of evolution and expansion for us—expansion of knowledge, influence, power and happiness.

If you're not passionate about an activity, it means that activity isn't providing you with growth, satisfaction, joy and expansion. Passion and success are inseparable to me. Passion is born of success—and the progress that comes with success.

Chris: Do you think people have innate passions, that even before they're successful at something, they have things they're just drawn irresistibly to?

Dr. Hagelin: They're drawn to them because when they tasted them, when they sampled that activity, they immediately experienced growth and progress in that direction. Typically, it's where their talent lies. It's a natural channel of creativity for them.

Chris: What role has that played in your life?

Dr. Hagelin: Passion has been absolutely key to me and, I would predict, key to everybody. Passions are the core of everyone's life. You are drawn to do things—to follow your passions—because that activity brings you expansion, joy and evolution.

Chris: In your own life, how has pursuing those things you're passionate about affected your health, wealth and spirituality?

Dr. Hagelin: The pursuit of my passions nourishes and sustains my life. By its very nature, it brings joy, success, health and happiness. I don't, and most people don't, continue to do things that don't bring success, achievement, progress and happiness.

Perhaps I'm a little more alert to this principle and choose those activities that are bearing fruit—fruit in terms of progress towards achievement, which brings happiness and sustains life.

Pursuit of passion is so basic to life, so intimate to life, that if you're not pursuing your passions, you're not going to be happy for long. You're not going to be able to sustain that direction for very long. Yet one does have control, to some extent, over what constitutes one's passion.

What you put your attention on grows stronger in your life. You can culture an interest for something. You can develop a talent in an area, which then allows you to succeed in that area, and thus enjoy progress, success and evolution through that channel. That area will become more and more of a passion for you when your activity in that area rewards you with joy, progress, expansion and evolution.

People do have freedom—and it's probably the greatest human freedom—over what they give their attention to. And that area will become more central, more important in their life. I would recommend everyone exercise that freedom—to put their attention on projects that are truly worthy, with the potential to bring maximum happiness and evolution to their life and to society as a whole. The more global and far-reaching the project, the more happiness and evolution that project could potentially bring.

We have control over what might become a passion for us, and that's an important freedom we exercise. But there are obviously constraints on what could ever become our passion, based upon our core predispositions and genetic makeup.

Probably, although I enjoy art, painting will never become a passion for me: I am so utterly lacking in talent in that area that an effort in that direction would almost certainly meet with more frustration than joy. If I had some talent, if I were even moderately talented, I could nurture that talent, enjoy initial spurts of progress, and that could ultimately grow into a passion for me.

So we have some control, but there are constraints based upon our own, individual natures. Not everyone is going to be a great teacher. Not everyone is going to be a great politician.

In my life, I made choices to develop new areas, new passions that weren't, frankly, that natural to me—talents I wasn't born with. I was not born a quantum physicist: I was born an engineer.

Chris: And yet, some have called you one of the greatest quantum physicists of our age.

Dr. Hagelin: Yes, some have, and that did not come easily. I was born an engineer. When it came to classical physics, the laws of mechanics, I didn't have to study them. I knew them, they were in my bones, they were part of my genetic make up. But when it came to quantum mechanics, I had entered a strange new realm that was absolutely non-intuitive to me.

I should say, in fairness, quantum mechanics is counter-intuitive to most people. You have to rely solely on your mathematical abilities to delve into these abstract realms for which our intuition provides no guidance. And I wasn't a born mathematician. I had to really develop those skills over a period of years before I gained a natural fluency with the quantum world, and began to tackle problems in that world with increasing ease—and finally I gained some spark of fulfillment. It took time to develop that new channel of creative intelligence, that new channel of progress and satisfaction. It took time to build that new passion.

Chris: John, you have gone from what some people would consider one extreme to the other—from the rarified realm of theoretical quantum physics as one of the very top physicists in the world, to running for President of the United States.

Dr. Hagelin: That's the second example of creating a new passion, of developing myself in an area where I wasn't endowed with God-given talent, for the sake of the higher calling of service to humanity. Public policy didn't light my fire before I undertook this calling to evolve better principles and policies to govern our country and the world. I dove into the area of public policy, health care reform, etc., and relatively quickly, in comparison to quantum physics, found myself in a position of being able to make important, original contributions to these fields.

It's not rocket science, you could say. It's not quantum physics. It didn't take that long to expose the fallacies of our current policies in such areas as defense, which is based on offense, or health care, which is based on disease care, and so forth—and to construct more life-supporting policies that are in harmony with

natural law and make more efficient, compassionate use of our precious resources.

So this is another example of how my deepest sense of responsibility caused me to actually nurture and build a whole new passion, which then became the driving force of my life for quite a
few years.

Chris: Much of your professional life has dealt with the relationship between human consciousness and the deepest under-
standings and expressions of physics. Could you, for our readers'
benefit, talk a little bit about your understanding of consciousness,
its relationship to the physical, material world, and why it has
been such a key and important element in your life and your work?

Dr. Hagelin: As a young seeker of knowledge, I always strove
to understand the core reality of life, the truths of existence. What
I came to learn after fifteen years of higher education is that the
material universe is built upon the non-material quantum-
mechanical world of abstract intelligence that underlies it. The
exploration of deeper levels of natural law at the atomic and
nuclear and sub-nuclear levels was probing deeper levels of intelligence in nature that were far beyond the realm of material existence.

Ultimately, the discovery of the unified field, or heterotic
superstring, was a discovery of a field of pure intelligence whose
nature was not material, but pure, self-interacting consciousness.
So physics, in effect, had discovered consciousness at the foundation of material existence.

I wanted to know the nature of that consciousness, and it was
through Maharishi's programs, through his techniques for the
development of consciousness, that I experienced the reality of
what that field of consciousness is. I discovered for myself that
human intelligence, at its core foundation, is universal intelligence, and at that level, you and I and everyone and everything in

the universe are one.

We are united at our core, and that truth, that ultimate truth of the unity of life, is the most precious and crucially important understanding to emerge in this scientific age. This is the same reality that has been celebrated since time immemorial in all the great spiritual traditions of the world. But now this same truth is open to objective verification through the empirical approach of modern physics, and open to personal verification through the experiential approach of consciousness, and specifically for me, through the very universal and powerful technologies of Maharishi's Vedic science, including the Transcendental Meditation® program.

Chris: We believe strongly in the power of intention to manifest outcomes. What would you say is your current most important project, and what intention would you like us at *Healthy, Wealthy nWise*, as well as our readers, to hold for the fulfillment of that?

Dr. Hagelin: Firstly, I should say I strongly support your belief in the power of intention, based upon both science and direct experience. My most ardent desire today is to see an end to the senseless violence and continual legacy of war that has confronted humankind for so many, countless generations, and to bring lasting peace to the world on the basis of the emerging global understanding of the essential unity of life.

If all of us could own that vision, if all of us here could deeply understand and experience the unity of life, that unity will be far more easily understood and assimilated by the billions of citizens of our global family.

We are almost at the point where these words, where the ultimate reality of the unity of life, is resonating with people, beginning to make sense to people. We're not quite there, and it's important we nucleate the transition, that we precipitate the transformation by bringing this core understanding and experience to as many people as possible. And from that understanding and experience of unity, real, lasting peace will inevitably dawn in the world today.

Chris: Your responses have been very profound and have taken us to some of the deepest considerations of human life. What is the single most important idea you'd like to leave our readers with that we haven't yet discussed?

Dr. Hagelin: We've touched on it, but I think it's important to say. There's really no limit to human potential and there's no limit to what we can effortlessly achieve. The secret is to align human intelligence with the vast, organizing intelligence of nature that governs the universe and upholds millions of species here on earth and trillions throughout the universe.

By aligning our desires with the natural evolutionary flow of universal intelligence, virtually any impulse of thought can meet with tremendous success. Aligning individual intelligence with nature's intelligence is what is called "enlightenment."

Developing the total brain and rising to higher states of consciousness is absolutely key to achieving individual fulfillment, and is the key to contributing maximum to the evolution of society towards an enlightened society—a unified field-based civilization of peace, prosperity and harmony in the family of nations.

To learn more about the Institute of Science Technology and Public Policy, the Transcendental Meditation® program and the work of Dr. John Hagelin, visit:

www.istpp.org   www.tm.org
www.permanentpeace.org   www.hagelin.org

What were the key lessons from this interview about living your passion?

1. The core nature of life is to progress and evolve toward fulfillment.

2. When we're progressing and evolving, we experience joy, energy, vitality and health.

3. Activities through which we grow, through which we expand in knowledge, power, fulfillment: that type of activity brings joy.

4. When we're passionate about something, it's because it brings us joy, because that activity is a path of evolution and expansion for us.

5. If you're not passionate about an activity, that activity isn't bringing you growth and expansion.

6. Passion is born of success and the progress that comes with success.

7. Pursuit of passion is so basic to life that if you're not pursuing your passions, you're not going to be happy for long; you're not going to be able to sustain that direction for very long.

8. You have control over what might become a passion for you, within the constraints of your core predispositions and genetic makeup. You can culture an interest for something, or develop a talent in an area, which allows you to succeed in that area and that area will become more of a passion.

9. The greatest human freedom is the freedom over what you give your attention to. That area will become more central, more important to your life.

10. Your deepest sense of responsibility can cause you to nurture and build whole new passions.

11. The material universe is built on the non-material quantum-mechanical world of abstract intelligence that underlies it.

12. There is no limit to human potential, and no limit to what we can effortlessly achieve. The secret is to align human intelligence with the vast, organizing intelligence of nature.

13. By aligning our desires with the natural evolutionary flow of universal intelligence, any impulse of thought can meet with tremendous success. Aligning individual intelligence with nature's intelligence is what is called "enlightenment."

How will you use these points in your own life starting now?

You can be part of the live teleaudience, absolutely FREE, when Healthy Wealthy nWise conducts interviews with amazing people like the one you just read. Go to:

http://www.healthywealthynwise.com/interview

There you can quickly and easily sign up to receive reminders on all of the incredible upcoming calls.

EPILOGUE

You are not here merely to make a living. You are here in order to enable the world to live more amply, with greater vision, with a finer spirit of hope and achievement. You are here to enrich the world, and you impoverish yourself if you forget the errand.

—Woodrow Wilson

"How was your trip?" Chris asked.

"It was absolutely the best and most amazing experience of my entire life." Janet replied.

What will the best and most amazing experience of your life look like? By now we hope you understand you have the power to craft that experience.

You are creating your life and your world, every moment. Want to see how powerful you are? Look at your life.

Your life today is the result of the predominant thoughts you have held up until now. If you want your life to change, change your mind. It doesn't have to take a long time.

If you have completed the exercises we've introduced you to in this book, then you have a pretty good idea of what you choose to create. Now, it's just a matter of remembering:

What you put your attention on grows stronger in your life.

What will you put your attention on now? What did you learn from Janet's story?

Here are a few of the things we hope you picked up:

- Your life won't look the way you think it will.
- Get clear on the "what" and the "how" will begin to appear.
- Your challenge is to stay open, to let go of your concepts about how your life should be, and embrace the way it is.
- You will know you are aligned with your passions when things happen to you which others would find uncomfortable, distasteful, or undesirable, and they don't even faze you because you are so driven by the fire inside.
- Be prepared to find blessings coming to you from situations and circumstances which may at first appear to be the opposite (e.g. Janet's stepmother's passing or her altitude sickness in the Himalayas). Learn to look for the blessing.
- It takes courage to follow your own path. Surround yourself with people who support you in following your dreams. Avoid spending time with people who try to destroy them.
- Passion is a journey, not a destination. Every day choose in favor of your top passions, and you will soon find yourself living a passionate life.
- When you love the doing, the results will take care of themselves.
- Life is here to enjoy. The purpose of life is the expansion of happiness. When it appears otherwise, you are off the path of destiny. Look at your life and ask, "What do I need to change, to choose in favor of my passions?"

We have treasured this time with you. It's hard to say good-
bye. We hope you'll choose to say hello instead.

Join us for our Passion Series interviews. Send us your stories
of living your passion, so we can post them to inspire and motivate
others. You can send them to our attention at:

support@healthywealthynwise.com

Whatever you choose to do, remember the power and
strength of love. The things you love the most, those things we
call passions, are drawing you irresistibly on to the fulfillment of
your destiny.

We leave you with this thought:

Passion is born of love.
Love is the perfection of the divine in us.
Love lives, breathes
and finds expression through us
and fills us with the fire of passion.
Fulfillment arises from love,
and through love.

Let us live in love, for love's sake.
Let us be in love
and share our love
In the service of our common destiny.
Let passion emerge from us as love,
In the service of humanity.

♥

ARE YOU READY
FOR THE NEXT STEP?

FREE Special Report:

"Eight little-known secrets every wealthy person uses— and how they practically guarantee your success..."

Turn your passion for *anything* into profits you're proud of...

Please don't close this book saying "Wow! What a great book!" Though that would be flattering to us, what we really want is to help you take the next step and turn your passion into a profitable, wealth-producing, and fulfilling life.

That's why we've created a powerful 32-page Special Report designed to help you easily and effortlessly take the next step.

We've studied many of the world's most successful, wealthy, passionately happy people, harvesting their knowledge and learning the key principles they've used to create great wealth doing what they love doing.

We want you to have this information, so you can benefit from it right away and begin getting the same results.

In this FREE Special Report you'll learn how to:

- **Turn your passions into a raging river of profits (why not do what you love <u>and</u> make lots of money?)...**

- Turn mere dreams into **realities** (once you know this secret, everything becomes easy)...

- **Tap into an infinite source of creative ideas, allowing you to *solve any problem* and *successfully deal with any challenge* (there's a hidden part of you that knows just what to do in any situation—learn to quickly and easily find and utilize this source of wisdom)...**

- Attract super-successful mentors with the advice, wisdom, and experience you need to create the success you want (why reinvent the wheel, when successful mentors are just waiting to help you?)...

- **Tap into the networks of influential, connected people (this easy entrée into truly "fast lane" success can help you succeed ten, twenty—even fifty times—faster)...**

- Develop the little-known (but absolutely crucial) systems, skills, and tools used by the super-successful (they don't teach this in any school we know of, but once you know it, success becomes almost automatic)...

- **Create a huge passive income stream (learn the secrets of earning big money even while you sleep)...**

- Why the truly prosperous freely give huge amounts of time and money to the world—and how you can use this secret to create a richer and more fulfilling life...

- **And, a lot more!**

This Special Report is FREE to you, because you were wise enough to read *The Passion Test*™—and because we truly want you to have all the benefits we've talked about.

It's easy to get this Special Report. *You can be reading it and benefiting from it in just five minutes.* Just visit:

www.healthywealthynwise.com/report **right now and it's yours!**

So now it is time to close this book and say to yourself "Wow! What a great book!" Then, while you're thinking about it, go to:

www.healthywealthynwise.com/report

Get your FREE copy now of "Eight little-known secrets every wealthy person uses—and how they practically guarantee your success."

RESOURCES

In our experience, living your passions is a lot easier when you have help. Below are some of the people and organizations we have found who provide programs and services which can be of immense help on the path of passion. There are many more good programs in the world. These are a few of the best people and organizations we've experienced.

Expanding Awareness, Deepening Your Experience of Life

Transcendental Meditation® (TM) Program—We have both been practicing this powerfully effective program of deep meditation for over thirty years. We consider it the foundation on which everything else is built. It's simple, it's easy to do, it works and it complements every other practice. Over 600 scientific studies have been done on the benefits of TM. Be prepared to make an investment which will return to you many times over in innumerable ways. (**www.healthywealthynwise.com/tm**)

The Work of Byron Katie—Byron Katie (affectionately known as "Katie') is a remarkable woman who "woke up" to reality many years ago. In the process, she experienced an incredibly powerful and easy process of investigation which she now teaches throughout the world. The Work will allow you to systematically and effortlessly unravel the concepts which keep you from living your

greatness. It was a huge turning point in allowing us to deal with our challenges.
(www.healthywealthynwise.com/thework)

The Sedona Method—We've all been told the value of "letting go." The Sedona Method is a simple yet profound practice for doing just that. There is no limit to what you can accomplish or create in your life when you are able to truly let go of the emotions and concepts which hold you back.
(www.healthywealthynwise.com/sedona)

Centerpointe Research Institute—In the 70's, research found that sine waves in various forms could produce predictable changes in brain wave patterns. Bill Harris of Centerpointe Research used this knowledge to create the unique Holosync audio technology which creates the brain wave patterns associated with deep meditation. Holosync users report a broad spectrum of benefits in all areas of their lives. If you have had trouble with traditional meditation practices, this may be the solution you've been looking for. (www.healthywealthynwise.com/centerpointe)

Building the Foundation of Self-Knowledge

The Canfield Training Institute—Jack Canfield, co-creator of the *Chicken Soup for the Soul*® series is one of the best trainers in the world today. He will take you to new places in yourself and allow you to see the greatness in you. If you can't do any other trainings this year, do Jack's.
(**www.healthywealthynwise.com/canfield**)

Bob Scheinfeld's Busting Loose From the Money Game—If your aim is to go beyond creating wealth, to breaking free from the money game, you have to take this program. "Secrets" is a bit over-used in the marketing world, but this program really will unveil some core secrets about the nature of reality. Chris took this program and said it turned his world upside down. Prepare to have your mind blown. When you're finished, you'll understand what real freedom is and be starting to live it.
(**www.healthywealthynwise.com/bustingloose**)

Agape International Spiritual Center—Founded by Dr. Michael Beckwith in 1986 with fifteen members, today there are over 10,000 members and thousands attend services each Sunday. Non-denominational, Agape is an experience you don't want to miss if you are ever in Los Angeles, California. You'll experience the most inspiring music, loving community, and sermons by Rev. Michael which will transfix, motivate, and transform you. Words cannot begin to describe the experience of Agape. You have to experience it. (**www.healthywealthynwise.com/agape**)

The Kabbalah Center—You've heard about The Kabbalah Center from the news articles about their famous students, Madonna and Guy Ritchie, Demi Moore and Ashton Kutcher, among others. What you may not know is that Kabbalah's ancient teachings are immensely practical and applicable to building the life you have dreamed about.
(**www.healthywealthynwise.com/kabbalah**)

Bill Bauman—We sometimes refer to him as "the enlightened Mister Rogers." Funny, perceptive, inspiring, and thought provoking are all words which describe Bill. His courses, retreats and community of friends can be an incredible support when you need to surround yourself with people who will encourage you to fully express who you are.
(www.healthywealthynwise.com/billbauman)

The Unstoppable Cynthia Kersey—She wrote the book on being *Unstoppable*, she is mobilizing the unstoppable women of the world, and she is the living embodiment of what it means to be unstoppable. If you are committed to creating a whole new fulfilling, abundant life, then take Cynthia's 90-day challenge and become unstoppable!
(www.healthywealthynwise.com/unstoppable)

Dr. John DeMartini's Breakthrough Experience—John DeMartini's trainings are worth attending just for the pleasure of sitting with such a brilliant mind. From quantum physics to the mechanisms by which you create your reality, John will hold you spellbound. Then be prepared to do some serious inner work. Expect to come out of his courses transformed. You will be.
(www.healthywealthynwise.com/demartini)

Money and You—Excellerated Business Schools—In the next section on Creating Wealth you'll read about the brilliance of Marshall Thurber. Marshall created Money and You over 30 years ago. It is now run by D.C. Cordova and is still one of the most powerful courses available. While the title is about money, the content is a series of experiential games which will show you who you really are. Tony Robbins, Robert Kiyosaki, T. Harv Eker, Jack Canfield, Mark Victor Hansen, Spencer Johnson and many others have gone through this course before achieving their success. Think *you* might learn something there?
(www.healthywealthynwise.com/moneyandyou)

Attracting Perfect Customers—Jan Stringer and Alan Hickman will teach you a systematic process for attracting whomever you want into your life, from perfect customers, to the perfect relationship, to the perfect employee, to the perfect business partner. We use their process with every major initiative we take. It works. (**www.healthywealthynwise.com/perfectcustomers**)

Destiny Training Systems—Do you know you live in an abundant universe, but don't know how to access that abundance? Scott deMoulin's Destiny Training will show you how. Teaching practical, proven strategies for achieving true inner and outer wealth, Scott and his partner Dallyce have a huge following of raving fans. (**www.healthywealthynwise.com/destinytraining**)

Soulwave—The daughter of British physicists drafted to build the nuclear bomb to stop Hitler, Kathryn Darling grew up in the world of science. Today she teaches her students how to surf the natural flowing waves of life that connect you instantly to the flow of everything you need to be happy. If you're ready for "radical optimism," learning the meaning of true surrender, and transformations which could save your life, you are ready for Soulwave. (**www.healthywealthynwise.com/soulwave**)

James Ray International—"Balance is bogus! Harmony is what leads to happiness and real wealth," says self-made millionaire and master trainer James Ray. His "Journey to Power" course draws on his broad experience in traditional business and in the ancient cultures of Peru, Egypt and the Amazon jungle. He considers himself a "practical mystic" and in our experience he is a trainer who will challenge you, entertain you, sometimes shock you, and by one means or another, wake you up to the power that resides inside you. (**www.healthywealthynwise.com/jamesray**)

Creating Wealth

Marshall Thurber's Positive Deviant Network—Marshall studied and worked with both Nobel Laureate R. Buckminster Fuller and W. Edwards Deming, often credited with the transformation of Japanese industry in the 60's and 70's. Marshall is a genius in his own right. When Chris took Marshall's "Success Secrets of the 21st Century" he says it packed more valuable business learning in two days than the three years of his MBA program. If you have a business (large or small), and are ready to take it to another level, take this course. This is the leading edge of business knowledge. (**www.healthywealthynwise.com/thurber**)

T. Harv Eker's Millionaire Mind Intensives—He wrote the book on having a millionaire mind (*Secrets of the Millionaire Mind*), and he's one of the best trainers we've ever experienced. His courses are fun, challenging and incredibly rewarding. You will be an empowered, fearless person when you emerge. Get a copy of Harv's great book and, as of this writing, you'll receive two free tickets (worth $2,590) to his three day, Millionaire Mind Intensive, a course you do not want to miss. If you're just getting started on the path to financial wealth, this is the place to begin. (**www.healthywealthynwise.com/eker**)

Robert Allen and Mark Victor Hansen's Enlightened Millionaire Institute—We can't say enough good about our former partners. Popularly known as the Protégé program, The Enlightened Millionaire Institute provides practical, hands on courses, and will teach you the ins and outs of creating wealth through real estate, stocks, internet marketing and Infopreneuring (marketing information). The initial investment is substantial. The results you'll get when you apply yourself will be even more substantial. (**www.healthywealthynwise.com/emi**)

Raymond Aaron's Monthly Mentor—Famed for his financial success in Canada, author of *Chicken Soup for the Parents Soul* and *Chicken Soup for the Canadian Soul*, Raymond Aaron's Monthly Mentor program is not to be missed. Every month he interviews incredible people and gets them to spill their guts about what it takes to be successful. From Robert Kiyosaki to Mark Victor Hansen to Brian Tracy to Randy Gage, Raymond has a loyal following for good reason. (**www.healthywealthynwise.com/aaron**)

One Coach—The founders of One Coach, John Assaraf and Murray Smith, have made millions, repeatedly, in a variety of businesses. Now they are focused on helping the small business owner and entrepreneur with under $1 million in sales. Their program will coach you through the obstacles and challenges, while helping you identify the opportunities. What we love is the holistic approach they take to your success.
(**www.healthywealthynwise.com/onecoach**)

BNI (Business Networks International)—Founded by Dr. Ivan Misner, over 20 years ago when he wanted to generate more business for his consulting practice, BNI has grown to over 80,000 members and 4,000+ chapters. Allowing one member of each "flavor" (doctor, lawyer, hairstylist, chiropractor, etc.) per chapter, BNI members come together regularly to share referrals with each other. Based on the philosophy that "givers gain," last year alone BNI members exchanged over two million referrals and generated more than a billion U.S. dollars in business for each other. (**www.healthywealthynwise.com/bni**)

Stephen Pierce—If your path to wealth is through the internet, prepare to learn from one of the best. From search engine strategies, to launching a book, to ebay auctions, to getting publicity, Stephen is one of the top in the field of internet marketing. (**www.healthywealthynwise.com/pierce**)

Success University—This is one place you can go to get trained by the greatest mentors on creating wealth in the world. You'll take courses with Jim Rohn, Zig Ziglar, Brian Tracy, Les Brown, Jay Abraham, and many more. This unique resource is based on a network marketing model so you can learn and earn at the same time. (**www.healthywealthynwise.com/successu**)

Wildly Wealthy Women—This incredibly successful program from "down under" is soon coming to North America. Sandy Forster and Dymphna Boholt have created a program exclusively for women teaching them asset management, nothing down real estate strategies, safe stock market investment strategies and a host of other practical skills in a safe environment created by women for women. (**www.healthywealthynwise.com/wildlywealthy**)

Health

The Healing Codes—Twelve years of prayers were answered when the healing system he now calls "The Healing Codes" appeared to Dr. Alex Loyd and cured his wife's severe depression when nothing else would. As he applied The Healing Codes to the psychological and emotional issues of his clients, he was taken aback when they started reporting their recovery from serious health issues like multiple sclerosis, leukemia, Lou Gehrig's disease and others. Dr. Loyd is a wonderful, loving man. If health is an issue, The Healing Codes could create a miracle in your life. (**www.healthywealthynwise.com/healingcode**)

Ayushakti: Dr. Pankaj and Smita Naram—You've read some of his story in *The Passion Test*™. He is called on to take the pulse of the Dalai Lama, Mother Theresa praised him for his work, he has treated over 400,000 patients with outstanding results, and he has Ayurvedic Centers in twelve countries around the world. Dr. Naram comes to the U.S. twice a year and travels to Europe, Australia and other parts of the globe regularly. He is a remarkable man and an incredible source of healing knowledge. (**www.healthywealthynwise.com/naram**)

Master Stephen Co and Pranic Healing—Master Co is the author of *Your Hands Can Heal You*. He has been praised by Dr. Deepak Chopra, Marianne Williamson, Carolyn Myss, Mark Victor Hansen and many others for the power of his healing work. His active practice is teaching people how to heal themselves. (**www.healthywealthynwise.com/stephenco**)

Sri Sunil Das—Janet described some of the remarkable experiences she had with Sri Sunil Das in Part 1 of *The Passion Test*. Royalty, politicians, leading musicians, actors and actresses, as well as tens of thousands of Indians with all kinds of maladies come to Sri Sunil Das for healing. He is humble, kind, fun and insists all the healing which happens through him is "God's will." (**www.healthywealthynwise.com/sunildas**)

Master Chunyi Lin—Author of the #1 best seller, *Born a Healer*, Chunyi insists that anyone can heal themselves. He is a master of the ancient arts of Qigong, and his book is a good place to start in understanding how to heal yourself. His Spring Forest Qigong is offered through Learning Strategies Corporation (*see Other Resources below*) as a powerful self-study program. (**www.healthywealthynwise.com/chunyi**)

Amazon Herbs—"More than a company. A way of being in the world," is Amazon Herbs' motto. How often do you connect with a company that is committed to your personal health and lifestyle goals? A company that honors nature and indigenous culture? A company that lives a successful model of ecological prosperity every day and is the best at what they do? Amazon Herbs brings the healing medicinal herbs of the Amazon rain forest into your life. (**www.healthywealthynwise.com/amazon**)

Relationships

Dr. John Gray—What is there to say about the man who wrote the best-selling relationship book of all time, *Men are From Mars, Women are From Venus?* John offers a wide variety of resources to support men and women in creating healthy, fulfilling relationships. (**www.healthywealthynwise.com/marsvenus**)

Gay and Katie Hendricks—Co-founders of the Spiritual Cinema Circle, Gay and Katie have been supporting the creation of loving, fulfilling relationships in everyone who connects with them since they fell in love over 25 years ago. They have trained coaches throughout the world to bring hope, love, and the experience of unity to people everywhere.
(**www.healthywealthynwise.com/hendricks**)

Paul and Layne Cutright—Paul and Layne, best selling authors, coaches and teachers, have been in a romantic and creative partnership since 1976. They have taught tens of thousands of people the world over their secrets and strategies for successful relationships at home and in business.
(**www.healthywealthynwise.com/paulandlayne**)

Stephany Crowley's Edating Secrets—Internet dating is becoming one of the best ways to find your perfect partner. After all, Chris found his romantic partner through the internet. But it can be scary, uncertain, and a mammoth waste of time if you don't know what you're doing. Stephany wrote the book on *E-dating Secrets* and her programs can make you an internet dating expert in no time. (**www.healthywealthynwise.com/edating**)

Family and Kids

Lisa Nichols' Motivating the Teen Spirit—She's worked with over 50,000 "at risk" teens and helped more than 2,000 avert suicide. She is one of the most powerful, warm, straight forward speakers and trainers we have met. If you have teens, you will want to connect with Lisa. (**www.healthywealthynwise.com/teens**)

SuperCamp and Quantum Learning—SuperCamp has become famous for its powerful effect on kids and parents alike. It is based on concepts that make learning fun and easy, along with positive peer support and carefully orchestrated environmental factors. The use of metaphors like board breaking and ropes courses help students surpass barriers that hold them back. SuperCamp is ideal for both kids and families to do together. Programs are offered throughout the U.S. and worldwide. (**www.healthywealthynwise.com/supercamp**)

Other Resources

Learning Strategies Corporation—Paul Scheele and Pete Bisonnette have created powerful tools for learning a variety of useful subjects using accelerated learning, preconscious processing and neurolinguistic programming. Their products are outstanding. From Spring Forest Qigong to Diamond Feng Shui to Photo Reading to accessing your Genius Mind, to their Memory Optimizer, to just about anything you want to improve on, Learning Strategies has some of the best learning tools available anywhere. (**www.healthywealthynwise.com/learningstrategies**)

ConsciousOne—Want access to incredible authors and transformational leaders? At ConsciousOne you can read articles, listen to recordings and purchase products from people like: Neale Donald Walsch, Dr. Wayne Dyer, Doreen Virtue, Sylvia Browne, Gay and Katie Hendricks, Barbara Marx Hubbard and Jean Houston. (**www.healthywealthynwise.com/consciousone**)

SelfGrowth.com—This is another mother lode of resources in the field of personal growth and development. Among many other things, you'll be able to get founder David Riklan's compilation of *The Top 101 Experts That Help Us Improve Our Lives*. There are articles, event calendars and much more at this very useful web site. (**www.healthywealthynwise.com/selfgrowth**)

Spiritual Cinema Circle—Receive inspirational, uplifting films every month as a member of Spiritual Cinema Circle. These are chosen from the best short and feature films shown at festivals around the world, and most, while excellent, you would never see otherwise. Every month includes at least one full length feature, along with several shorter outstanding films. (**www.healthywealthynwise.com/scc**)

The Lefkoe Institute—From overcoming your fear of speaking to facing change to becoming a better parent to improving your golf game, Morty Lefkoe has created powerful processes for eliminating the beliefs which hold you back. Morty and his Certified facilitators have had incredible success working with people with a wide variety of issues including eating disorders, depression, violent behavior and stress, among many others. (**www.healthywealthynwise.com/lefkoe**)

Coachville—The largest association/network of coaches in the world, Coachville brings together over 40,000 coaches. If you're interested in becoming a coach or connecting with coaches, this is the place to go. (**www.healthywealthynwise.com/coachville**)

Doing Life!®️ International—A 2004 study documented that her programs had saved State of New York taxpayers over $1 billion. Dr. Cheryl Clark has spent 30 years applying the wisdom of R. Buckminster Fuller to social situations through "Social Synergetics." The Social Synergetics™️ model for successful living integrates Physical, Mental, Emotional and Spiritual components of human existence and offers a ground-breaking framework for lives and relationships that are vital, nourishing, creative and joyful. (**www.healthywealthynwise.com/doinglife**)

ACKNOWLEDGEMENTS

As with every book, many people have made it possible. Our partners at Healthy Wealthy nWise, Ric and Liz Thompson, have been incredible. Every crazy idea we have which makes at least a modicum of sense, they have supported. They chose to share their magazine with us, and then have worked shoulder to shoulder as together we have created a unique online resource which allows everyday people to spend time with and learn from some of the most amazing people in the world. Ric and Liz, thank you first and foremost for your friendship, and for creating the online systems to allow so many people to gain the knowledge they need to live their destinies.

Mark Victor Hansen and Robert G. Allen, thank you for who you are. You showed us that the door marked "Security" isn't secure at all, and the door marked "Freedom" is a lot more fun, if a bit hair raising at times. And thank you for being open to our idea of putting "enlightened" and "millionaire" together, so we can all begin to realize spirituality and wealth are complimentary, not mutually exclusive, ways of living life.

Harv Eker, Jack Canfield, Paul Scheele, Pete Bisonnette, Bill Harris, Michael Beckwith, Byron Katie, Jay Abraham, Pankaj and Smita Naram, Bill Bauman, and Tom Painter, we are so grateful for our friendship, and for your generosity in sharing your knowledge, your experience and your wisdom.

Marci Shimoff, what an extraordinary friend and counselor you have been. Your love, wisdom and practical advice have been indispensable. Thank you for reminding us of who we are.

Bill Levacy, thank you for your profound jyotish guidance and amazing ability to take three simple words, "intention, attention, no tension" and give so much clarity to them that our lives and our readers lives will forever be transformed.

Sylva Dvorak, Pat Burns, and Melony Malouf thank you for being the best of friends—always there, always ready to support us when we really need it. You are so special to us.

Christina Collins Hill, your jyotish skills have been so important in helping us "avert the danger which has not yet come." Thank you for your continued love and support in all that we do.

Chris Strodder, thank you for your patience in reading and rereading this book so many times. Your suggestions, questions, and comments have made the final version so much richer. Liz Howard, you are a miracle worker. Thank you for doing such a beautiful job in designing the book, and for doing it in record time.

George Foster, what a treat you are to work with, play with and laugh with. Your sense of humor combined with your incredible design skills have made you one of our ideal partners. We are excited to help the world know you're the one to go to when they need an amazing book cover.

From Janet: I'm so thankful to all the great Masters who opened their hearts and minds, and in many cases, their homes, so I could both fulfill my passions, and share their wisdom with so many.

To my Angel group, Mo, Sue, Suzanne, Cindy, Tony, Jerrie, Deb Sue and Sandy, thank you for always being my cheering squad! Even if your minds couldn't always wrap your arms around what I was up to, your hearts always did.

To Mickey and Johnny, my dear sister and brother, what a

blessing you are in my life. It's so amazing to know that whatever happens, you will always be there for me. Thank you for your encouragement, for your love, and for helping to pick me up when the road got tough.

Christian Seaton, thank you for being the best friend a girl could ever want, all these many years.

Radhika Schwartz, Martin Gluckman, and Krishna thank you for pointing me in the direction of the wisest people on the planet. Martin, I'm so grateful to you for traveling with me on parts of my journey. Juliann Jannus, thank you for your flexibility in leaving your job to travel across the world with me, and thank you for getting me started on my video career.

Debra Sue Poneman, you started me on this journey, almost thirty years ago. Thank you for your inspiration, your wisdom and for making the world of transformation look like so much fun!

To Ashoklal, Bindu, Krishna and Debu, and to Kannan, Amita, and the rest of my Indian family, thank you for taking such good care of me and making sure I had a home away from home.

Glory be Chris…what haven't we been through together?! Thank you for teaching me that "if it isn't fun, I don't want to play." Thank you as well for your incredible ability to bring out the greatness in everyone around you. It's an honor to be your best friend and business partner.

To my dear parents and beloved Margie, I am what I am because of you. Thank you for pushing me to be my own person.

From Chris: My dear beloved Doe, what a blessing you are in my life. Thank you for your patience with me through the late nights, early mornings and weekends it took to get this book done. Your continued love and support mean everything to me.

Mom and Erich, thank you for showering me with your love. Mom, thank you for always encouraging me to follow my own direction, even when you thought it was completely nuts.

Dear Dad. What a life we had together, huh? Thank you for allowing me to feel so loved. This book is as much yours as it is mine. Thank you for showing me what courage really looks like.

Rolf and Renee Erickson, what amazing friends you are. Thank you for your excellent feedback. Bob and Patricia Oates, I am so grateful for you both. Bob and Rolf, thank you for sharing so many incredible passionate adventures with me, so I actually have an idea what it means to live passionately.

Mark Schoenfeld, thank you for your friendship, and for reminding me of what is real. To all my buddies on the Purusha program, in the U.S., Europe and in the high mountains of the Himalayas, thank you for your silence, your dedication, and the powerful effect of coherence you are having on the world.

And Janet, what a remarkable teacher you are. You have helped me transform my life into more than I could ever have dreamed. It's so unbelievable to know there is someone who will never give up on me, who I can always depend on, who will do whatever it takes. You are my inspiration, my best friend and my perfect partner.

And lastly, on behalf of both of us, we cannot begin to give words to the deep gratitude we feel to His Holiness Maharishi Mahesh Yogi for giving us the direct experience and understanding of the most fundamental nature of reality. We feel deeply blessed.

ABOUT THE AUTHORS

Co-founders of online magazine *Healthy Wealthy nWise* and partners in Enlightened Alliances, a marketing consulting firm, Chris and Janet Attwood regularly spend time with some of the greatest transformational leaders interviewing them on their passions. Their Passion Series interviews have helped thousands of people learn the principles which lead to a passionate life. They've interviewed people like: T. Harv Eker, Neale Donald Walsh, Byron Katie, Stephen R. Covey, David Lynch, Dr. Wayne Dyer, John Gray, and others.

Chris and Janet were once married, but are no longer, yet they remain best friends and business partners. After many successful years in the corporate world, they gave up the security of their well-paid jobs to partner with Mark Victor Hansen and Robert Allen to create The Enlightened Millionaire Program. They are founding members of Jack Canfield's Transformational Leadership Council and active members of Marshall Thurber's Positive Deviant Network. When not traveling to the far reaches of the globe in pursuit of their passions, they both live in Mill Valley, California.

Janet Attwood is a master communicator and connector. She has always had the gift of connecting with people, no matter what their status or position. From the influential and powerful, to the rich and famous, to the Saints of India, Nepal, the Philippines and elsewhere, to lepers and AIDS patients and anyone who is seeking to live their destiny, Janet bonds with every one.

She has been the top salesperson at every company she has worked at over the past twenty years and ran the Marketing Division of Books are Fun, the third largest book buyer in the U.S. In the year after her division posted record sales, Books are Fun was sold to Reader's Digest for $380 million.

Janet has been practicing the Transcendental Meditation® program for thirty-seven years and is a facilitator of the Work of Byron Katie.

Chris Attwood is an expert in the field of personal development. For over thirty years he has studied and explored the field of human consciousness. In the 80's he spent more than ten years in deep meditation and has extensively studied the Vedic tradition of India.

He has also put his theoretical knowledge to practice. Chris is skilled at consultative sales and management. Over the past 27 years he has been President, Chief Operating Officer, General Manager, or CEO of ten companies. He has sold millions of dollars of consulting and training to organizations like Dell Computer, Royal Bank of Canada, Sprint, Ford Motor Company, Mellon Bank, and others.

Janet and Chris are committed to the experience and expression of the unlimited potential of the heart and mind. They teach, and their daily practice is, what it means to live a life of unconditional love.

♥